THE WAY
PEOPLE
LIVE

Life in a
Medieval Castle

THE WAY
PEOPLE
LIVE

Life in a
Medieval Castle

Titles in The Way People Live series include:

Cowboys in the Old West
Games of Ancient Rome
Life Among the Great Plains Indians
Life Among the Ibo Women of Nigeria
Life Among the Indian Fighters
Life Among the Pirates
Life Among the Samurai
Life Among the Vikings
Life During the Crusades
Life During the French Revolution
Life During the Gold Rush
Life During the Great Depression
Life During the Middle Ages
Life During the Renaissance
Life During the Russian Revolution
Life During the Spanish Inquisition
Life in a Japanese American Internment Camp
Life in a Medieval Castle
Life in Ancient Athens
Life in Ancient Greece
Life in Ancient Rome
Life in an Eskimo Village
Life in a Wild West Show
Life in Charles Dickens's England
Life in the Amazon Rain Forest
Life in the American Colonies
Life in the Elizabethan Theater
Life in the North During the Civil War
Life in the South During the Civil War
Life in the Warsaw Ghetto
Life in Victorian England
Life in War-Torn Bosnia
Life of a Roman Slave
Life of a Slave on a Southern Plantation
Life on a Medieval Pilgrimage
Life on an Israeli Kibbutz
Life on the American Frontier
Life on the Oregon Trail
Life on the Underground Railroad

THE WAY
PEOPLE
LIVE

Life in a
Medieval Castle

by Gary L. Blackwood

Lucent Books, P.O. Box 289011, San Diego, CA 92198-9011

Library of Congress Cataloging-in-Publication Data

Blackwood, Gary L.
    Life in a medieval castle / by Gary L. Blackwood.
        p.   cm. — (The way people live series)
    Includes bibliographical references (p.   ) and index.
    Summary: Describes the history, purpose, and construction of medieval
castles and the life of their various inhabitants.
    ISBN 1-56006-582-6 (lib. bdg. : alk. paper)
    1. Castles Juvenile literature.   2. Civilization, Medieval Juvenile
literature.   [1. Castles.   2. Civilization, Medieval.]   I. Title.   II. Series.
GT3550.B58   2000
940.1—dc21   99-26848
                                                                                            CIP

Copyright 2000 by Lucent Books, Inc., P.O. Box 289011, San Diego, California
92198-9011

Printed in the U.S.A.

Contents

FOREWORD
Discovering the Humanity in Us All   8

INTRODUCTION
The Feudal Family   10

CHAPTER ONE
The Rise of the Castle   15

CHAPTER TWO
A Town Within Walls   24

CHAPTER THREE
Lifestyles of the Rich and Noble   34

CHAPTER FOUR
The Lives of Women and Children   45

CHAPTER FIVE
A Soldier's Life   56

CHAPTER SIX
Life Among the Lowly   67

CHAPTER SEVEN
Life in Wartime   77

EPILOGUE
The Decline of the Castle   89

Notes   93
For Further Reading   97
Works Consulted   98
Additional Works Consulted   101
Index   102
Picture Credits   107
About the Author   108

Discovering the Humanity in Us All

Books in The Way People Live series focus on groups of people in a wide variety of circumstances, settings, and time periods. Some books focus on different cultural groups, others, on people in a particular historical time period, while others cover people involved in a specific event. Each book emphasizes the daily routines, personal and historical struggles, and achievements of people from all walks of life.

To really understand any culture, it is necessary to strip the mind of the common notions we hold about groups of people. These stereotypes are the archenemies of learning. It does not even matter whether the stereotypes are positive or negative; they are confining and tight. Removing them is a challenge that's not easily met, as anyone who has ever tried it will admit. Ideas that do not fit into the templates we create are unwelcome visitors—ones we would prefer remain quietly in a corner or forgotten room.

The cowboy of the Old West is a good example of such confining roles. The cowboy was courageous, yet soft-spoken. His time (it is always a he, in our template) was spent alternatively saving a rancher's daughter from certain death on a runaway stagecoach, or shooting it out with rustlers. At times, of course, he was likely to get a little crazy in town after a trail drive, but for the most part, he was the epitome of inner strength. It is disconcerting to find out that the cowboy is human, even a bit childish. Can it really be true that cowboys would line up to help the cook on the trail drive grind coffee, just hoping he would give them a little stick of peppermint candy that came with the coffee shipment? The idea of tough cowboys vying with one another to help "Coosie" (as they called their cooks) for a bit of candy seems silly and out of place.

So is the vision of Eskimos playing video games and watching MTV, living in prefab housing in the Arctic. It just does not fit with what "Eskimo" means. We are far more comfortable with snow igloos and whale blubber, harpoons and kayaks.

Although the cultures dealt with in Lucent's The Way People Live series are often historically and socially well known, the emphasis is on the personal aspects of life. Groups of people, while unquestionably affected by their politics and their governmental structures, are more than those institutions. How do people in a particular time and place educate their children? What do they eat? And how do they build their houses? What kinds of work do they do? What kinds of games do they enjoy? The answers to these questions bring these cultures to life. People's lives are revealed in the particulars and only by knowing the particulars can we understand these cultures' will to survive and their moments of weakness and greatness.

This is not to say that understanding politics does not help to understand a culture. There is no question that the Warsaw ghetto, for example, was a culture that was brought about by the politics and social ideas of Adolf

Hitler and the Third Reich. But the Jews who were crowded together in the ghetto cannot be understood by the Reich's politics. Their life was a day-to-day battle for existence, and the creativity and methods they used to prolong their lives is a vital story of human perseverance that would be denied by focusing only on the institutions of Hitler's Germany. Knowing that children as young as five or six outwitted Nazi guards on a daily basis, that Jewish policemen helped the Germans control the ghetto, that children attended secret schools in the ghetto and even earned diplomas—these are the things that reveal the fabric of life, that can inspire, intrigue, and amaze.

Books in The Way People Live series allow both the casual reader and the student to see humans as victims, heroes, and onlookers. And although humans act in ways that can fill us with feelings of sorrow and revulsion, it is important to remember that "hero," "predator," and "victim" are dangerous terms. Heaping undue pity or praise on people reduces them to objects, and strips them of their humanity.

Seeing the Jews of Warsaw only as victims is to deny their humanity. Seeing them only as they appear in surviving photos, staring at the camera with infinite sadness, is limiting, both to them and to those who want to understand them. To an object of pity, the only appropriate response becomes "Those poor creatures!" and that reduces both the quality of their struggle and the depth of their despair. No one is served by such two-dimensional views of people and their cultures.

With this in mind, The Way People Live series strives to flesh out the traditional, two-dimensional views of people in various cultures and historical circumstances. Using a wide variety of primary quotations—the words not only of the politicians and government leaders, but of the real people whose lives are being examined—each book in the series attempts to show an honest and complete picture of a culture removed from our own by time or space.

By examining cultures in this way, the reader will notice not only the glaring differences from his or her own culture, but also will be struck by the similarities. For indeed, people share common needs—warmth, good company, stability, and affirmation from others. Ultimately, seeing how people really live, or have lived, can only enrich our understanding of ourselves.

The Feudal Family

For the first four centuries following the birth of Christ, most of Great Britain and western Europe was under the control of the Roman Empire. From time to time, the Celtic tribes who had inhabited Britain and France for several hundred years rose up in revolt. But the Roman army was so efficient that it kept even the far reaches of the empire in a state of relative peace, stability, and prosperity, sometimes called the *Pax Romana,* or "Roman peace."

Then, in about the third century A.D. the Roman Empire began a slow political and economic decline. So-called barbarian tribes— the Vandals, the Huns, the Visigoths, and the Franks—took advantage of the empire's weakness to invade it from the East. As the Roman armies withdrew from France and England to defend the heart of the empire, those countries, too, were invaded by the Franks, the Picts, the Saxons, and finally the Vikings.

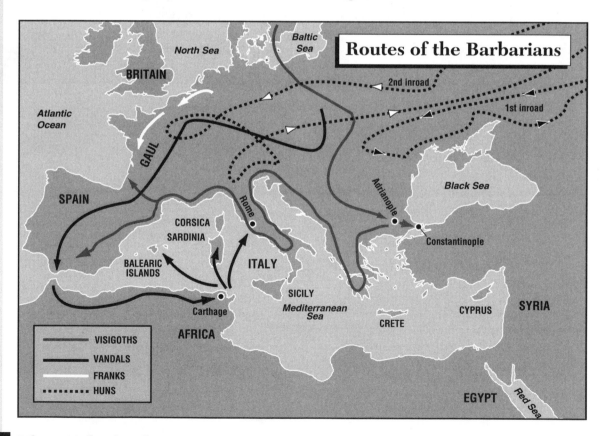

Routes of the Barbarians

North Sea
Baltic Sea
BRITAIN
2nd inroad
Atlantic Ocean
1st inroad
GAUL
Adrianople
Black Sea
SPAIN
Rome
CORSICA
SARDINIA
Constantinople
BALEARIC ISLANDS
ITALY
Carthage
SICILY
Mediterranean Sea
CYPRUS
SYRIA
AFRICA
CRETE

VISIGOTHS
VANDALS
FRANKS
HUNS

EGYPT
Red Sea

"To the inhabitants who protested and pleaded for help," writes historian Morris Bishop, "the Roman emperor replied that they must learn to take care of themselves."[1] Individual leaders, one of whom was no doubt the model for the legendary King Arthur, brought temporary order to some areas, but the widespread authority of the Pax Romana was shattered.

As scholar Barbara W. Tuchman writes,

> After the Empire's collapse, the medieval society that emerged was a set of disjointed and clashing parts subject to no central or effective secular authority.[2]

Power and Protection

This lack of a strong central government, as author Marc Bloch points out, made life uncertain and hazardous, both for the common people and for the "nobles"—those who had a measure of wealth and power:

> Neither the State nor the family any longer provided adequate protection. . . . Everywhere, the weak man felt the need to be sheltered by someone more powerful. The powerful man, in his turn, could not maintain his prestige or his fortune or even ensure his own safety except by securing for himself . . . the support of subordinates bound to his service.[3]

A new social arrangement was needed that would satisfy both the desire of the weak person to be protected and the desire of the strong person for support. Over a period of several centuries, such an arrangement developed in the form of feudalism.

The term *feudalism* probably was not coined until sometime in the seventeenth

Racing from the East, the fierce Huns invade the Roman Empire, slaughtering indiscriminately along the way.

century, but the system it describes was in force far earlier. In Germany, for example, a young warrior traditionally pledged loyalty and service to an older, more experienced one in return for guidance and protection. Likewise, Roman citizens received patronage and protection from influential men in exchange for allegiance. And, according to writers Clara and Richard Winston,

From the earliest times Frankish chiefs had gathered household aides and fighting men around themselves. These were their "men" or "vassals." . . . Essentially a pact was made, with the vassal undertaking certain fixed obligations, especially to defend the lord with his body. In return the lord promised protection and economic maintenance.[4]

Order and Organization

By the tenth century, the Normans of northwestern France, who had a gift for administration and law, were fine tuning the feudal system. Under their rule, what had been an ill-defined set of loyalties became a well-ordered system that was, according to Bishop, "simple and logical":

> The king kept a part of his realm as his own demesne [estate], which he farmed and administered for his own support. The rest he entrusted to his faithful companions in the form of fiefs [grants]. . . . In return for his land the noble became his lord's vassal, owing to him services, particularly the provision of a fixed number of armed horsemen for his lord's wars. The noble, vassal of his king, was also a lord, empowered to grant a share of his land, with its accompanying rights and duties, to a vassal of his own.[5]

The *grands seigneurs,* the wealthiest barons who were direct vassals of the king, usually were given the title of duke, count, or marquis. The lesser nobles, to whom the *grands seigneurs* granted fiefs, were smaller barons or ordinary knights. Their parcel of land, accordingly, was sometimes known as a "knight's fee." This system was based on

A knight or baron might be granted a fief not just by one lord but by several different ones. This, of course, created conflicting loyalties. When the vassal took an oath, he might have to include in it all sorts of conditions and reservations.

French knight John of Toul had feudal ties to no fewer than five greater nobles, including the count of Champagne and the count of Grandpré. The complicated oath he took is recorded by Jay Williams in *Life in the Middle Ages.*

"If it should happen that the count of Grandpré should be at war with the countess and count of Champagne I will aid the count of Grandpré in my own person, and will send the count and countess of Champagne the knights whose service I owe to them for the fief which I hold of them. But if the count of Grandpré shall make war on the countess and the count of Champagne on behalf of his friends and not in his own quarrel, I will aid in my own person the count and countess of Champagne, and will send one knight to the count of Grandpré for the service which I owe him for the fief I hold of him, but I will not go myself into the territory of the count of Grandpré to make war on him."

land because, in a time of economic instability, land represented the only real wealth.

Over time the terms of the feudal contract became more and more specific. A knight's fee became defined as enough land to yield a yearly income of at least twenty pounds. The knight was required to have on hand a warhorse and suitable weapons and armor. Instead of owing his lord an unspecified term of service, the vassal was obliged to serve only for a fixed period, usually forty days each year.

Manors and Monasteries

The lands granted to barons and knights were, in turn, rented out to tenant farmers. Though some of these tenants, called serfs, were required to labor in the local lord's fields for a certain number of days each year, they were not his vassals. And they were not, strictly speaking, part of the feudal system.

The relationship between a local lord and the serfs and freemen who worked the land belonging to him is usually known as the manorial or seigneurial system. This system, which was based on agriculture, was in place long before feudalism, which was essentially military in nature.

The church, however, was a part of the feudal system. It owned vast tracts of land. Bishops and abbots became vassals of the king and the great lords. Some of the clergy even fulfilled their military obligations. Three French bishops fought the English at Poitiers in 1356; the archbishop of Sens was killed in battle at Agincourt.

Fathers and Sons

Despite the legal qualities of the feudal system, it was essentially family-like in nature. The lord was a father figure; the vassals were equivalent to sons. According to French historian Georges Duby, "It was their duty to love the lord under whose banner they fought, just as young men loved the father of a family."[6]

A vassal kneels while paying homage to his king. In return for the vassal's loyalty and service, the king would provide guidance, protection, and land.

The bond between lord and vassal was cemented not by some businesslike contract but by a ceremony that was very personal. This ritual, known as homage—from the French word *homme,* meaning "man"—is described by Morris Bishop:

The vassal knelt, placed his clasped hands within those of his master, declared, "Lord, I become your man," and took an oath of fealty. The lord raised him to his feet and bestowed on him a ceremonial kiss. The vassal was thenceforth bound by his oath "to love what his lord loved and loathe what he loathed, and never by word or deed do aught that should grieve him."[7]

The more vassals a noble had, obviously, the greater his wealth was, the larger his power base, and the more soldiers he had at his command. But the obligation went both ways. As his vassals owed him military duty, he owed them patronage and protection. This meant maintaining a seat of authority, preferably a fortified one where individual knights could gather and make a united stand against invaders or against rival bands of knights. It meant, in other words, having a castle.

The Rise of the Castle

"The development of feudalism," writes historian Joan Evans, "is reflected in the development of the castle."[8] In the ninth and tenth centuries, when warring factions in Europe were numerous and relatively small, castles were small and simple affairs, meant mainly to provide a place for a lord and his knights to hole up temporarily when they were under attack.

But as the size of the great lords' feudal "families" grew, so did their castles. They were transformed from temporary fortresses into full-time living quarters. In fact, a castle is, by the usual definition, designed for more than just defense. It is also meant to be a home. It is, in other words, a fortified residence.

The Earliest Castles

Castles of various sorts were common throughout Europe during the Middle Ages—in Belgium, Switzerland, the Netherlands, Germany, and Italy. They served a variety of purposes: as toll stations, arsenals, fortresses, and watchtowers. In terms of a fortified residence, the castle flourished above all in those countries where the feudal system was most firmly in place—in France and in Norman-occupied Britain.

The Normans were originally a Viking people from Norway who made frequent raids on western France during the ninth century and finally settled there permanently in the district named for them—Normandy. Before the Norman invasion, European fortifications were crude for the most part, not much more than a ring of mounded-up earth surrounded by a ditch and topped by a fence, or palisade, of upright logs.

In the first half of the tenth century, structures that could properly be considered castles began to appear. They were of this same basic "ringwork" design, except for the addition of a tower, or donjon, sometimes inaccurately called a keep. The donjon provided a stronghold that was more secure and could be more easily defended than the palisade.

Building the Motte and Bailey

Jean de Colmieu, writing in the early twelfth century, describes how such a castle was constructed:

> They throw up a little hill of earth as high as they can; they surround it by a fosse [ditch] of considerable width and awful depth. On the inside edge of the fosse they set a palisade of squared logs of wood. . . . If it is possible they strengthen this palisade by towers built at various points. On the top of the little hill they build a house, or rather a citadel, whence a man can see on all sides. No one can reach its door except by a bridge, which . . . gradually rises until it reaches the top of the little hill and the door of the house, from which the master can control the whole of it.[9]

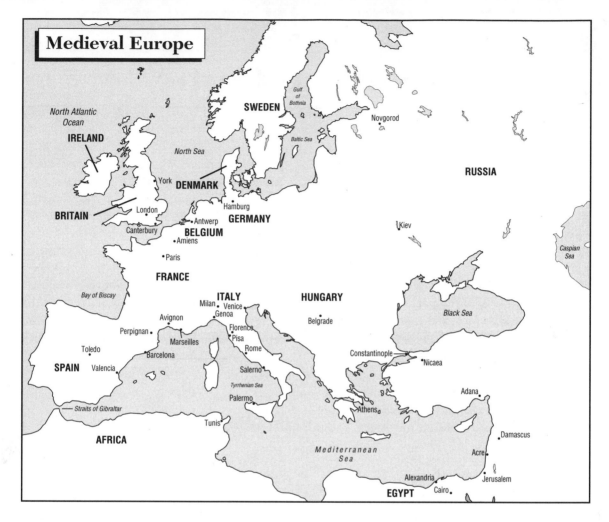

Medieval Europe

North Atlantic Ocean

IRELAND

BRITAIN

York

London

Canterbury

North Sea

DENMARK

SWEDEN

Gulf of Bothnia

Baltic Sea

Novgorod

RUSSIA

Hamburg

Antwerp

GERMANY

BELGIUM

Amiens

Paris

FRANCE

Kiev

Caspian Sea

Bay of Biscay

ITALY

Milan

Venice

Genoa

HUNGARY

Belgrade

Black Sea

Avignon

Perpignan

Florence

Pisa

Marseilles

Rome

Toledo

Barcelona

Constantinople

Nicaea

SPAIN

Valencia

Salerno

Adana

Tyrrhenian Sea

Palermo

Athens

Damascus

Straits of Gibraltar

AFRICA

Tunis

Mediterranean Sea

Acre

Alexandria

Cairo

EGYPT

Jerusalem

This fortified hill was called a motte, meaning "mound" in French (not to be confused with the word *moat,* another name for the ditch that was dug around the perimeter). Most mottes were 100 to 250 feet in diameter at the base and could be as high as 80 feet, not including the height of the tower, which might add another 30 or 40 feet.

The area within the palisade, which might cover from two to ten acres, was called the bailey. In some castles, the bailey entirely surrounded the motte. In others it was entirely separate, except for the wooden bridge described by de Colmieu that linked the two

sections. In this case, the motte might have a smaller palisade of its own around the tower.

Unless the builder took advantage of an existing rise in the ground, or built atop the ruins of an earlier fortification, constructing the motte was a long and grueling undertaking, often performed by forced labor recruited against their will from the surrounding countryside. A French parish priest named Lambert witnessed the building of an earthen fortification around the year 1200:

There, again, laboured the ditchers with their shovels, the hoe-men with their hoes, the pickers with their pick-axes . . . the catchpolls [guards] too, with their rods and knotted clubs, rousing the labourers and busily urging them to their work; and ever in the forefront the masters of the work, weighing all that was done in the scales of their geometrical plan; moreover, all these labourers were driven and constrained to this work through a continual time of travail [effort] and grief, of fear and pain.[10]

The Three-Story Tower

Depending on the number of workers, the building of the motte could occupy two or three weeks; construction of the palisade and tower might require an additional month. The tower, or donjon, was the heart of the castle. During a siege, it was the last line of defense. If the bailey was overrun, the garrison—the soldiers who occupied the castle—retreated to the donjon and shut the door against the besiegers. In the early days of the motte and bailey, the donjon also served as a residence.

An ordinary Norman manor house of the time had a simple floor plan: the kitchen and storeroom were located at one end, the main living and dining room was in the center, and the lord's private chamber was at the other end. The layout of the typical donjon probably resembled a manor house turned up on end, so that the kitchen was on the ground floor, the main hall on the second floor, and the lord's chamber at the top. Considering that the towers of many motte and baileys were no more than twelve feet square and forty feet tall, life inside them must have been cramped, to say the least.

Daunting Defenses

By the twelfth century most castle owners were following the fashion of building a more spacious and less spartan hall within the bailey

The fortified motte and expansive bailey are clearly visible in this reconstruction of an advanced Norman castle, which boasts stone rather than wooden stockades.

for everyday living and retreating to the dreary donjon only when it was absolutely necessary for defense.

By today's standards, a three-story tower made of wood does not seem all that secure. But the great siege engines that would come on the scene a century later for the purpose of battering down stone walls had not yet come into general use. The approved method of attempting to capture a castle was a direct frontal attack—usually an unsuccessful one. As historian N. J. G. Pounds writes, "One is struck by the ability of earthwork castles with their wooden defences to resist a powerful and sustained attack. . . . Their summits could have provided space for a sizable garrison, and their steep slopes might have been almost unscalable in the face of archers stationed on the summit."[11]

The Drawbacks of the Donjon

A tower made of timber did have one major shortcoming, of course—it could be set afire. The garrison did their best to prevent this by either splashing water on the walls regularly or by draping them with wet animal hides. Unfortunately, because the tower was built on an artificial hill, the supply of water was usually very limited. What little could be stored in the tower had to be conserved for drinking, in case of a prolonged siege.

The amount of provisions that could be stored there was limited, too. As a result, knowing that they could not hold out indefinitely, a castle's defenders might make the decision to surrender early on. Historian Anthony Kemp recounts a short-lived siege of a French motte and bailey in the year 1111:

After the defenders had been driven inside the castle, an attempt was made to storm the gatehouse of the bailey, and then to set it alight. Carts full of wood soaked in fat were pushed up, under a storm of missiles hurled by the garrison. The defenders managed to extinguish the burning carts, and they likewise repulsed an assault across the ditch and up the rampart. Finally, however, a breach in the palisade was made, forcing the garrison to retreat into the tower on the motte, where they shortly afterward surrendered.[12]

Even after stone castles began to make an appearance toward the end of the eleventh century, timber and earthen construction continued to be used because it was relatively quick and cheap, and it did not require much in the way of skilled labor.

Castles of the Conquest

The motte and bailey played a pivotal role in the invasion and conquest of England by William, duke of Normandy. When William the Conqueror landed on English soil in September 1066, one of his first acts was to build a castle near Hastings, where the decisive battle would take place. The construction was done mainly by Anglo-Saxon peasants pressed into service by the Norman soldiers. Soon after the conquest, according to twelfth-century historian Ordericus Vitalis,

the king [William] rode into all the remote parts of his kingdom and fortified strategic sites against enemy attack. For the fortifications, called castles by the Normans, were scarcely known in the English provinces, and so, the English, in spite of their courage and love of fighting, could put up only a weak resistance to their enemies.[13]

quest was, in the words of historians H. G. Richardson and G. O. Sayles, "violent, bloody, and disorderly."[14]

Towers of Stone

Many of these castles were of the old motte-and-bailey type, with timber palisades and donjons. But wealthier barons, knights, and lords had begun to build more durable towers of stone. Some attempted to modify an existing motte and bailey by building a stone structure atop the motte or a masonry wall to replace the wooden one. This type of converted motte and bailey was called a shell keep. The conversion often proved to be a disastrous mistake, though. The mounded earth had a tendency to shift and slump, taking sections of stone wall with it. Builders quickly learned that, if they wanted their stone structures to last, the foundations needed to be sunk down to bedrock or at least laid on a deep trench filled with rocks.

The earliest stone castles consisted of a freestanding donjon or great tower, which, because of its small perimeter, was far easier for a garrison of limited size to defend. Like the wooden towers that preceded it, the typical stone donjon was square or rectangular, but many builders preferred a cylindrical tower because a round design was sturdier and cheaper to build, and because it had no corners that could be undermined.

Putting Up Obstacles

Though stone towers tended to be larger overall than timber ones, much of that size was in the walls, which might be twelve feet thick or even more. So these new donjons shared one major drawback with the old ones—a serious

William the Conqueror is credited with introducing fortified castles to England as well as mounted warriors and a complex feudal system.

Along with the strategic value of the castle, William introduced two other influential concepts to England. One was the use of mounted warriors in battle. The other was a highly structured feudal system, with the Norman lords placed securely on the top rungs of the social ladder.

Land was taken from the hands of the Anglo-Saxon lords and bestowed upon two hundred or so of William's closest companions in arms. These barons and knights wasted no time in building protective castles on their fiefs since the period that followed the con-

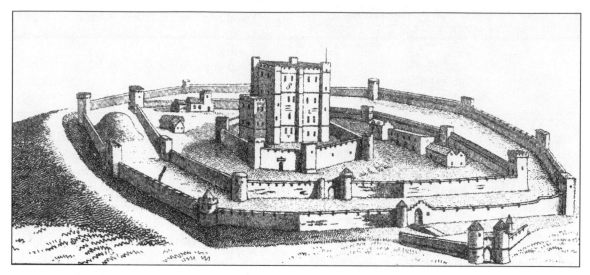

Concentric fortifications surround an elaborate Norman castle, ably protecting the stone donjon from invading armies.

lack of space. The garrison could not possibly pack all their possessions into the tower, certainly not their horses and livestock. Like the wooden tower, the stone donjon needed a bailey surrounded by a protective wall that formed the first line of defense.

If one encircling wall was good, it stood to reason that two would be even better. English and French soldiers had learned just how effective a design using multiple walls, called concentric fortification, could be when they attacked the fortified towns of the Middle East during the First Crusade (1096–1099). In the twelfth century, the principle of concentric fortification started to come into its own in the crusaders' home countries. England's famous Tower of London is one of the earliest concentric castles in Europe.

A castle of this kind was beyond the means of ordinary knights and barons. Constructing even a simple freestanding donjon could set the builder back as much as two thousand pounds; at the time, the majority of nobles earned less than one hundred pounds a year from their estates, and a baron with an annual income of one thousand pounds was considered enormously wealthy. A more elaborate fortification was likely to cost from ten thousand to twenty thousand pounds—more than the king himself took in each year.

The Art of Castle Building

Ordinarily the cost of building a castle was spread out over a period of several years, for the construction of thick walls of stone and mortar was a laborious process. If the walls were laid up stone by stone using mortar made of burned lime and sand, they might rise at a rate of only ten feet or so per year. A faster method, borrowed from Saracen castle builders in Spain, involved building a low temporary wall of wooden planks and then pouring between the boards a mixture, or aggregate, of mortar and small rocks. Usually this rough wall was then faced with an outer "skin" of cut stone to make it more attractive and less vulnerable to attack. Frequently, the stone surface was whitewashed with lime.

In theory, masons, carpenters, and laborers received a daily wage that ranged from three pence to twelve pence per day. In practice, because there was often not much hard money in circulation, their pay might consist, at least in part, of food, drink, or clothing. There was always a certain amount of coin available, though, as Urban Tigner Holmes Jr. explains in *Daily Living in the Twelfth Century.*

"At the time all money in France and England was in silver pennies, or 'deniers.' . . . Higher values of money were made by weighing out scoopfuls of these deniers at the money-changer's. A 'marc' was eight ounces. . . . A 'livre' was a pound of twelve ounces. . . . A 'sou' was twelve deniers.

According to the English monetary system, the equivalent of the denier was the penny, a shilling (12 pence) was equivalent to the sou, and a pound (240 pence or 20 shillings) was the same value as the livre."

A silver penny issued by William the Conqueror portrays the king's likeness.

There were few professional architects. Castles were, for the most part, designed and their construction supervised by master masons who had learned their trade on the job, working for another master mason on some other castle.

The only machinery at the mason's disposal was the wheelbarrow and a simple pulley-wheel crane with a basket for hoisting materials into place. Even with a large force of laborers on hand, building a decent-sized donjon and fortified enclosure could take seven or eight years. In rare cases, when speed was the overriding factor and money was no object, builders might hire a vast number of workers and manage to throw up a defensible stone castle in a matter of a few months.

As the art of castle building improved and the donjon, instead of standing alone, was surrounded by a stone wall that could be defended against attack, the owner no longer felt the need to hole up in a great tower for security. Instead, he built a spacious residential hall within the bailey and regarded the donjon only as a place of last refuge, in case the walls were breached. "Around the turn of the 13th century," writes historian Dominique Berthelemy, "it became possible both to withstand far more serious sieges and to live in greater comfort than ever before."[15]

A Fortress First

Though the comfort level of the typical castle may have improved, it still was not the most pleasant of dwellings. Historian Plantagenet Somerset Fry notes that

> of the hundreds of castles that remain . . . there are very few that give one any feeling that they could have been

One of the biggest problems involved in building a castle at a remote site was finding skilled workers to do the job. Most castle builders brought in masons and carpenters from outside the area, sometimes even from other countries. Marjorie Rowling elaborates on these traveling workers in *Everyday Life of Medieval Travelers.*

"Throughout the Middle Ages craftsmen connected with the building trade, whether master masons, mere hewers and quarriers, artists, sculptors, carpenters or smiths, were mostly itinerant [traveling]. . . . As they so often had to tramp from place to place to reach their building sites, they often put up at wayside inns and doubtless, finding convivial company, stayed unduly long at some. This [French poet] Christine de Pisan had described.

> At these taverns every day
> You will find that they will stay,
> And go on drinking far too long,
> Until it gets to evensong.
> By which time they've spent, it's true,
> More than they'd earn a long day through."

An innkeeper serves food to a trio of workers. Numerous laborers and artisans were needed to construct a castle, and the crew often found respite in such inns and taverns.

Workers often had to rely on brute strength when constructing castles like this one, which was built along England's busy Tyne River in 1080.

comfortable places to live in. . . . And yet for feudal lords there was no alternative. . . . They lived in an era of warfare . . . and they had perforce to organize their lives around a permanent capability for defending themselves. . . . [A lord's] building, therefore, had to be a combination of fortress and residence and generally it had to be fortress first. That meant sacrificing much in the way of softer surroundings.[16]

Barbara W. Tuchman sums it up more succinctly: "One governing concept shaped a castle: not residence, but defense."[17]

But warfare, of course, is more than just a matter of defense. Medieval barons were not simply a lot of victims sitting passively behind their fortifications waiting to be besieged; they were also the aggressors. They built their castles not just for personal protection but also as headquarters from which they could ride forth and attack rival barons. Jean de Colmieu, who lived during this era, offers this grim assessment of the role of castles: "Their purpose was to enable these men [knights], constantly occupied with quarrels and massacres, to protect themselves from their enemies, to triumph over their equals, to oppress their inferiors."[18]

2 A Town Within Walls

The main concern of the baron who was contemplating the construction of a castle was to ensure that he could hold out against a besieging force for as long as possible. Though the design of a castle was certainly an important factor, equally important was its location. The ideal site for a castle was atop an existing hill. Not only did this vantage point give the garrison a clear view of all approaches to the castle, it would effectively slow down an attacking force if it had to climb uphill. The site could not be too inaccessible, of course. The defenders had to be able to exit the castle readily, either to make a counterattack or, if all else failed, to make their escape.

Another favorite location was next to a river, preferably in a spot where the river formed a large loop, enclosing a piece of land with water on three sides—forming a natural moat. Lacking this, the builder could dig an artificial ditch and let the river fill it up.

A good source of water was a necessity for drinking, washing, bathing, watering livestock, and wetting down wooden structures during a siege to make them resistant to fire. Most castle owners also had a well dug inside the bailey so they would have a source of drinking water even if the castle was surrounded.

"An Economic Unit All by Itself"

Though some castles were built adjacent to large towns and could purchase goods and supplies from the local merchants, most were more isolated and had to be largely self-contained and self-sufficient in peacetime but even more so during a siege. The ideal fortified residence was, according to historian William Stearns Davis, "an economic unit all by itself. . . . The estate has its own corn lands and pasture, its stacks of hay, its granaries and storehouses, its mills, cattle byres, slaughter houses, and salting sheds. Practically every scrap of food actually needed in the castle is grown locally."[19] If an estate was well managed, it might even provide a surplus of produce that could be sold at market, adding to the income the lord received from rents and taxes. Not all households could provide for themselves quite so well, particularly the largest ones, which might play host to a constant stream of visiting nobles who needed to be fed and entertained. Still, those goods and services that the estate could not provide could usually be obtained within half a day's ride of the castle.

Stable and Smithy

"The castle was not a single structure," explains historian Margaret Wade Labarge, "but a series of separate buildings within a protecting wall."[20] In fact, the bailey of the typical country castle resembled a very compact town. An early description of Fotheringhay Castle in Northamptonshire, England, records a stone tower and a moat . . . a great hall, two chambers, two chapels, a kitchen and a bakery of stone . . . a grange, a granary, a great stable, a long house used for ox-house, cowhouse, dairy and larder; a forge and a house for the outer gate with a chamber above.[21]

This town within the walls was equipped to provide most of the essentials of everyday life and, in addition, all the elements necessary for warfare. In most castles, all these buildings were contained in an area of about fifty thousand square feet—roughly the size of a football field.

The two most conspicuous buildings with a military function were the stables and the smithy. Because horses were so essential to the waging of war, the stables were important structures and were often very extensive. One stable at Chester Castle in Cheshire, England, was so huge that twenty-one thousand slates were required to cover the roof.

The smithy, where the knights' horses were shod and where new weapons and armor were manufactured and old ones were repaired, was one of the busiest buildings—and by far the noisiest. A fourteenth-century poet complained that the blacksmiths and armorers

The epitome of a strong fortress, England's Nottingham Castle—depicted here during the sixteenth century—functioned as a town within walls.

Drive me to death with the din of their
dints;

Such noise on nights ne heard men
never . . .

Lus! bus! las! das! . . . Christ them give
sorrow!

May no man for brenn-waters [hissing of
hot steel in water] on night have his
rest.[22]

Another important structure was the
mews, which housed the hawks and falcons
the nobles used for hunting.

The Great Hall

The focus of life within the bailey, though,
was the great hall. Once the donjon was rele-
gated to a purely defensive role, the hall became the primary residence and the center of
the noble's life. In it, he held court, transacted
business affairs, entertained, and dined.

The term *great hall* was, in many cases,
an overstatement, for none but the richest
nobles could boast of having castles with
more than two or three rooms. The layout of
these rooms was essentially the same as it had
been in Norman manor houses for centuries:
kitchen, main living and dining room, and private chamber.

Private is probably an overstatement as
well, as Marc Bloch makes clear: "Day and
night, the baron was surrounded by retainers—
men-at-arms, menials, household vassals,
young nobles committed to his care as
'nurslings'—who served him, guarded him,
conversed with him and who . . . continued to
keep faithful watch over him even when he
was in bed with his wife."[23]

Often the master's bedroom was separated
from the main room only by a curtain. In a
larger hall, it might be enclosed by a wooden
or stone wall. In the castle of a wealthy noble,
the bedroom could be practically luxurious.
The walls might be plastered and whitewashed
with lime or painted with murals, paneled with
wood, or perhaps covered with hangings, usually ones of linen that was dyed a solid color.
By the fourteenth century the richest barons
were displaying the colorful, heavy woven tapestries that are associated with the Middle
Ages. The cold stone or tile floor might be
partly covered with imported carpets.

Bedroom furniture was sparse, usually
consisting of a wooden chest used to store
clothing and valuables, a bench or stool, a
candlestick, and a bed. The heavy wooden
frame of the bed was laced with rope or
leather thongs. On top of these was spread a
thick mattress, usually stuffed with feathers.
At night, linen hangings were pulled into
place around the bed to shut out the "un-
healthy" evening air. During the day, the
hangings were pulled back so the bed could
serve as an extra seat.

Light and Heat

Many chambers were undoubtedly gloomy.
To light the room after it grew dark, wealthy
castle owners used candles made of beeswax.
Those who could not afford this luxury used
candles of tallow—animal fat—which gave off
acrid smoke and a nasty smell. Two even
more unsatisfactory alternatives were the
rushlight, which consisted of bulrushes
dipped in tallow, and the cresset lamp, a
metal holder containing oil and a cotton wick.
Despite the smoke and odor, it was a common
practice to burn a candle in the bedchamber
all night long to keep away pixies and demons.

During daylight hours, the room was illu-
minated only by a small window or two; in

A lord and his household relax within their great hall, which also served as the dining room, seat of business, and dormitory.

winter these were closed up against the cold by wooden shutters, except in those households that could afford glass window panes. Labarge notes that, by the thirteenth century, "glass windows were becoming a great deal more common. . . . In fact, glass windows were rather more common and cheaper . . . than is generally recognized."[24] Still, they could be a major expense; often only half the window was glazed and the other half provided with a shutter.

If the room had no fireplace, it was heated in the cold months by a brazier full of burning charcoal, which must have rendered the air in the room practically unbreathable at times.

The Dormitory and Dining Room

A lucky attendant or two might sleep in the lord's chamber on a truckle bed—a low bed that slid out of sight under the larger one. But most members of the household slept along the walls in the main hall on straw mats laid out on benches or on the floor, which was usually strewn with rushes.

During the day this large sleeping room was transformed into a dining room by the addition of tables. The "upper" table, where the master and mistress and their high-ranking guests sat, was usually a permanent fixture of

Although medieval bedrooms were sparsely furnished, wealthy nobles decorated their chambers with extravagant tapestries, rugs, and linens.

the room. Often it was placed on a raised platform, or dais, at the end of the room that contained the fireplace. For the other members of the household, a "lower" table or two were set up on trestles, or wooden supports, at right angles to the upper table. Except for the lord and his wife, who occupied thronelike chairs, the diners sat on backless benches.

In many castles, just off the main hall were two small rooms: the pantry, where the bowls and silverware and linens were kept, and the buttery, which, despite what the name implies, was used for storing ale and wine.

"A Necessary Minimum of Sanitation"

The main hall contained several other small rooms with less appetizing functions. Except in royal residences and a few large monaster-

ies, there were no separate bathrooms as such. Most stone castles had built into the walls of the hall and the tower small niches called garderobes that were like indoor outhouses. They usually consisted of nothing more than a raised stone platform with a hole in it. The waste dropped through a drain shaft into a cesspool or into the moat, if there was one.

In the most up-to-date castles, the garderobes might be flushed out regularly with water piped in from a cistern, or water tank, in the tower. Ordinarily, though, the job was done by servants with buckets of water. Despite frequent washings, the smell from the garderobes likely lingered in adjacent rooms. Historian Urban Tigner Holmes Jr. comments that

the *odeur de merde* was never completely absent from anyone's nostrils. People were used to it; but we must not assume that nobody ever complained. There is a story told by Jacques of Vitry of a man whose job it was to clean out *garde-robe* pits. He did not mind the odor in which he worked all day, but his nostrils were badly offended by the smell of a snuffed candle.[25]

Toilet paper was, of course, unknown. Its role was filled by *torche-culs*—handfuls of straw or hay—or by a curved stick called a *gomphus*. Although this all sounds rather primitive and unsanitary by today's standards, Labarge points out that

contrary to modern misconceptions of medieval life, the upper classes particularly took considerable trouble to achieve what they considered a necessary minimum of sanitation. In fact their standards of personal cleanliness were much higher than those which prevailed from the sixteenth to the eighteenth centuries.[26]

In Hot Water

Medieval people also loved baths. The lord and his lady customarily bathed in their chamber in

Medieval Maladies

In spite of the castle owners' best efforts to keep themselves and their surroundings clean, the living conditions of the time contributed to a wide range of illnesses and afflictions. As Morris Bishop writes in his book *The Middle Ages*, "Polluted water, tainted foods, the rheumatic, pneumonic damp of stone-walled rooms, mistreatment of wounds, epidemics of typhoid, dysentery, smallpox, influenza and the plague took a heavy toll. The nobles consumed too much meat and alcohol, and in the winter no Vitamin C."

The lack of vitamin C led to scurvy, and the heavy diet was responsible for the widespread incidence among the nobility of gout, a painful inflammation of the joints and limbs that was known as "the malady of the rich."

Skin diseases were common, too, thanks in part to the predominance of wool clothing, which irritated the skin and held dirt. Because of the tendency of wool to shrink when washed, the household might send soiled clothing out to a tailor to have the dirty outer layer of the cloth shorn off.

Due to the often unsanitary conditions within a castle, as well as the dampness of its stone rooms, many castle dwellers suffered from illnesses such as influenza and dysentery or contracted diseases such as typhoid and the plague (pictured).

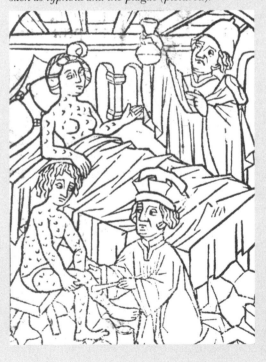

a wooden tub that resembled a barrel cut in half. The tub was filled with hot water carried in by servants. A stool might be set inside the tub for long soaks. If the bather was particularly modest, or the room particularly cold, a pole might be raised and a curtain draped over it, like a tent, for privacy and warmth. When the tub was not being used for bathing, it could be turned over and used as a table.

Gloomy Rooms

Most castles had an infirmary, a room where the sick received care. Today's doctors recognize the benefits of sunlight and fresh air, but the medieval sick ward was usually located in a dark interior room. In those days, as historian Davis notes, "every physician . . . will tell you that darkness is the friend of health and that few invalids can hope to get better unless they are kept as shaded and sequestered as possible."[27]

There was one room in the castle sure to be even gloomier than the sick ward: the cell where prisoners were kept. Such rooms were almost invariably cramped, sometimes just barely large enough for a man to stretch out full length on the floor. The humane ones might be on an outside wall and have a narrow slit that admitted a little light and air. But often cells were located beneath the floor and could be reached only by way of a trapdoor. These damp, dark dungeons were called oubliettes, from a French word that means "forgotten"—which accurately describes the plight of many a medieval prisoner. Not all were treated so harshly, of course. An enemy knight who was being held for a substantial ransom had to be kept healthy and happy; he was often given the run of the castle and shared the same accommodations and bill of fare as his captors.

Fear of Fire

The kitchen where the food was prepared might be part of the main hall, or for safety's sake, it might be in a separate building. Since meals were mainly cooked over an open flame, the kitchen was at considerable risk of catching on fire and burning to the ground.

The bakehouse, with its great dome-shaped oven, was usually in a separate building, too. The oven was heated by burning wood inside. The ashes were then raked out and the bread dough was placed on the hot floor. Obviously, the oven, too, was a serious fire hazard, and was usually isolated from the hall.

Fire was a constant concern throughout the castle because of the materials used in its construction. The donjon and great hall were likely to be made of stone and roofed with either slate or thin sheets of lead. To save expense, however, the lesser structures were built of wood and covered with wooden shingles or thatched with bundles of reeds, which were very flammable.

Built to Last

The one building on which most nobles spared no expense was the chapel. Religion played a bigger role in people's everyday lives than it does today, and, accordingly, virtually every castle had a house of worship; many castles had more than one. It could range in size and splendor from a small room adapted as a chapel to a whole separate building as large and well appointed as a parish church.

Whatever the size, most chapels were built to last. As Pounds writes, "Although some chapels were timber-framed, the great majority were not only masonry-built but were elaborately carved and decorated. . . .

Because food was normally roasted or cooked over an open flame, the kitchen was often separate from the main hall to prevent possible fires from enveloping the castle.

The interiors of most chapels were wainscoted and painted, the windows were glazed, and the floor tiled."[28]

By today's standards, of course, the buildings of even the most expensive, well-appointed castle would seem unappealing: cold in the winter; stifling in the summer; and dark, damp, and smelly all year round. But by the standards of the time, they were the height of luxury. Medieval folk, after all, were no more fond of ugliness and discomfort than today's society. Owners did all they could to make their surroundings as attractive and as livable as possible.

Gerald of Wales, a twelfth-century archdeacon and author, painted an almost idyllic picture of the small castle where he grew up:

It is excellently well-defended by turrets and bulwarks, and is situated on the summit of a hill . . . having on the northern and southern sides a fine fish-pond under its wall, as conspicuous for its grand appearance, as for the depth of its waters, and a beautiful orchard on the same side, inclosed on one part by a vineyard, and on the other by a wood, remarkable for the projection of its rocks, and the height of its hazel trees.

On the right side of the promontory, between the castle and the church, near the site of a very large lake and mill, a rivulet of never-failing water falls through a valley.[29]

Of course, how idyllic life in a castle—or anywhere else—might or might not have been depended largely on what place one occupied in the feudal structure.

"Some Work, Some Pray, Some Fight"

A popular theory of the time held that society was naturally divided into three distinct segments, or orders: the clergy, the nobility, and the common people. For each order life was quite different, and members had pre-

Ornate windows, wall paintings, and a glistening tile floor accentuate the importance of this small castle chapel.

Feudal Follies

Many of the castles of the wealthiest barons featured beautifully landscaped gardens where the lord and his lady could find a bit of peace and solitude—and, in some cases, a little amusement. Barbara W. Tuchman explains in her book *A Distant Mirror.*

"[Some nobles] built their 'follies,' of which the most elaborate were the mechanical practical jokes devised by Count Robert of Artois at the château of Hesdin. Statues in his garden squirted water on visitors when they walked past or squawked words at them like parrots; a trapdoor dropped the passerby onto a featherbed below . . . conduits under certain pressures 'wet the ladies from below.'"

scribed roles to play. A thirteenth-century poem makes the nature of the hierarchy clear:

> The cleric's job is to pray to God.
>
> Justice is the job of the knight.
>
> The laborer's job is to provide their bread.
>
> Some work, some pray, some fight.[30]

Jacques of Vitry, a medieval monk, compared all of humanity to a vast body in which the priests were the head and eyes, showing the way to the rest; the nobles were the hands and arms, protecting the body from harm; and the peasants, of course, were the legs, holding it all up. It is obvious which part of the body was best equipped to take what it wanted—and to hold onto it.

Lifestyles of the Rich and Noble

There was a good deal of variation, of course, within each of the three segments of society. The classification of clergy included everything from bishops and abbots whose lifestyles resembled those of wealthy barons, to the poorest monk who had renounced all worldly things.

The peasant class, at one extreme, consisted of wretched serfs who owned nothing, not even themselves; at the other extreme were prosperous, free yeomen farmers who owned sizable estates. The ranks of the nobility had to make room for all degrees, too, as Barbara W. Tuchman notes:

> Not all nobles were *grands seigneurs*. . . . They ranged from the great dukedoms with revenues of more than 10,000 livres [pounds], down through the lord of a minor castle with one or two knights as vassals and an income under 500 livres, to the poor knight at the bottom of the scale who was lord of no one except those of servile birth and whose only fief was a house and a few fields equivalent to a peasant's holding.[31]

A Certain Standard

Still, for the most part, nobles had more in common with one another than they did with those outside their order. They felt that, as aristocrats, a certain standard of living was expected of them, and they did their best to eat,

dress, and conduct themselves like nobility, even if they ran themselves irretrievably into debt doing it. Keeping a grand house, serving sumptuous meals, and having a large complement of servants and followers were all ways in which a lord could advertise his power, his wealth, his nobility.

In case any noble was not certain how to behave befitting his class, there was no shortage of advice from contemporary writers. A popular rhyme of the day advised, "Rise at five, dine at nine, Sup at five, to bed at nine Is the way to live to be ninety and nine."[32] A French treatise titled *Les quatre ages de l'homme* (*The Four Ages of Man*) recommends the following daily routine—as interpreted by historian Joan Evans—to a knight or baron who was not engaged in war at the moment:

> He is to begin with a triple sign of the Cross and prayer; then, before getting up, he is to think of what is to be done in the course of the day . . . and to repeat it to himself three times that he may not forget. Then he is to hear mass; to give alms, if only a little; to dress very carefully, and to see that his nails are clean; and then to proceed with his business diligently. At midday it should be finished, so that he may eat and drink in peace.[33]

There is no mention of breakfast here, for it was not a recognized meal. Most lords started

A bevy of servants attend to aristocratic diners at a fourteenth-century banquet. Hosting such luxurious feasts allowed nobles to showcase their elegant homes and large troupes of servants, both of which alluded to the lord's wealth and power.

the day with nothing more than a cup of wine and a chunk of bread, unless they were faced with some strenuous task, in which case they might fill up on a meat pie.

A Shave and a Haircut

Though the author of *Les quatre ages* cites clean nails as a priority, cleanly shaven faces were not. Common men customarily wore full beards, but facial hair had fallen out of favor among high-born men by the end of the twelfth century. A few days' growth was apparently acceptable, though, for most lords let their barber take a razor to them only two or three times a week. This is understandable considering the primitive state of the straight razor, which bore a close resemblance to a carving knife.

Regular haircuts were not a major concern, either. Most men let their hair grow down to just below the ears, but usually no longer, for fear of being considered effeminate.

Complicated Clothing

A respectable knight or baron was conscientious about his clothing. Until late in the fourteenth century, nobles tended to sleep without a stitch on, except perhaps a nightcap—an odd custom in view of how chilly castles could be in

In a castle, keeping track of the hours of the day was an inexact science at best. Mechanical clocks did not come into general use until the fourteenth century. An hourglass could measure only a relatively small segment of time. Sundials were reasonably accurate—but only when the sun was shining. For the most part, marking the hours was the responsibility of the clergy, who tolled the bell in the church, chapel, or monastery every three hours, more or less, throughout the day.

These intervals were usually calculated either by the length of time it took to recite certain prayers or by the amount the candles on the altar had burned down. Each observance of the hour had its own Latin name.

The day began with "lauds" at three A.M. "Prime" was rung at daylight, around six A.M., followed by "tierce," then "sext" at midday, then "nones," "vespers" at dusk, "compline" at bedtime, and "matins" at midnight.

Generally speaking, though, medieval folk were just not as concerned with time and its passage as people are today. Most likely the average castle dweller had but a vague notion of what year it was, let alone the hour or the minute.

---

winter. Upon rising, however, they made up for this lack of clothing by wearing as much clothing as possible.

Dressing could be a rather complicated affair; most lords were aided by an attendant known as "the first body squire." The first item of clothing to go on was the *braies*, a loose pair of underwear made of linen and fastened by a cloth belt. Next came the *chauces*, woolen stockings that were pulled up above the knee and kept in place by garters. The squire then slipped over the lord's head an ankle-length shirt called a *chainse*, which had long tight sleeves. Before buttons came into general use in the thirteenth century, the cuffs of the shirt were sewn together each time it was worn.

Over the *chainse* went a short-sleeved surcoat, or *bliaut*. On grand occasions the lord might wear a *bliaut* made of expensive silk, but for everyday wear he would choose one of cotton or fustian, a blend of cotton and flax or cotton and wool. The neck of the surcoat was held closed by a brooch or a pin, usually a quite showy one. The long narrow belt tied at the waist was often elaborate and expensive, too.

In cold weather a man of wealth wore a fur-lined tunic, or *pellice,* over his surcoat. For even more warmth, he might add a mantle, a circular cape usually made of wool and lined with the fur of squirrels or rabbits or perhaps with sheepskin, known as budge.

Wearing furs was practically a sign of nobility. So was the length of the *chainse* and *bliaut.* While a workingman's coarse tunic came only to his knees and a merchant's or clergyman's might reach to mid-calf, the nobleman made a point of wearing his to his ankles both to demonstrate that he did not have to work and to show that he could afford as much fabric as he liked.

One refinement that even the richest of nobles lacked was the pocket, which did not come into use until the sixteenth century. Men carried coins and other small items knotted up in one of their sleeves, in the hem of their *chainse,* or in a pouch or purse hung from their belt.

Setting an Example

Since the lord of a household was expected to set a good example, his first public act of the day was to attend mass in the chapel. Then, as *Les quatre ages de l'homme* suggests, he saw to it that a little of his wealth was handed out, either in the form of money or perhaps in clothing or shoes, to the poor gathered outside the castle gates. But, notes historian Kate Mertes, "Most lords had certain biases in their almsgiving. . . . The most frequent recipients of alms . . . were friars of one sort or another. Impoverished university students were frequently favored, and many lords were particularly charitable to lepers."[34]

High and Low Justice

The next order of the noble's day was to hold court at the table in the main hall, where he handled household business matters and dispensed justice. A great nobleman ordinarily had the right of the high justice; in other words, he held the power of life and death over everyone within his domain. A mere knight or petty baron was likely to have only the right of low justice, which allowed him to sentence common criminals.

Most of the cases brought before the lord were not matters of life and death, of course. Usually they involved settling disputes between the lord's vassals or disciplining some member of the household who had broken one of the castle's house rules. As Mertes explains, castle owners had regulations designed to

> prevent the waste or theft of food, embezzlement, theft of other items. . . . But a good many of the rules have to do with general behaviour. Gambling with dice or cards was forbidden . . . regulations against swearing were oft repeated . . . and tellers of ignoble stories, and "users of ribawdry [vulgar humor]," were also discouraged. . . . Drunkenness and fighting were also taken very seriously. For all these misdemeanors a first offence could earn a fine; a second several days' pay; and a third, dismissal from service. . . . Attendance at chapel was in all households supposed to

In addition to attending mass and distributing alms to the poor, a powerful nobleman was also expected to tend to household business and dispense justice.

be enforced by the exaction of penalties which could be either fines or even restriction of diet to bread and water.[35]

A more serious infraction of the rules might earn the offender a day on the pillory, a wooden scaffold where he or she was restrained by a wooden collar and subjected to the taunts of onlookers. Worse, he or she might receive a public flogging with a knotted rope.

Judge and Jury

Fellow nobles were, of course, not subject to such undignified punishments. For them, a fine was the usual form of discipline for relatively minor offenses. Clerics were not subject to the lord's justice at all; the church reserved the right to judge and punish its own.

The lord did not necessarily judge all the cases himself. If the matter was a relatively minor one, involving a serf or yeoman, he might delegate the responsibility to his steward or sheriff or some other official. When called upon to settle a more serious matter, most lords were not so arrogant as to rely solely on their own judgment. They often based their decisions on "custom law"—that is, how similar cases were handled in the past.

When custom law did not provide a satisfactory precedent, the lord might consult a clerk who had been schooled in the legal system used by the Romans. He might also employ an early form of trial by jury. This concept had been introduced into France and England by the Franks and was further refined by the Normans. According to a Muslim chronicler who recorded how the jury system worked, the lord

said to six, seven knights, "Arise and judge this case for him the defendant." The knights . . . retired by themselves and consulted together until they all agreed upon one thing. Then they returned . . . and said, "We have passed judgment to the effect. . . ." Such a judgment, after having been pronounced by the knights, not even the king . . . can alter or revoke.[36]

The Practice of Arms

After the official business was out of the way, the lord might make a tour of the castle grounds, inspecting the horses in the stables, checking on the work of the armorers, watching the knights and squires practice their battle skills—in short, making certain that when he and his vassals were called upon to take up arms, they would be ready. A lord never lost sight of the fact that his main occupation was not the management of a castle but the waging of war.

In fact, a noble who devoted too much attention to taking care of his estates was suspect, especially if he became concerned with making a profit from them. Honoré Bonet, a fourteenth-century cleric, cautioned that a knight should "have no cause to leave the practice of arms for the desire of acquiring worldly riches."[37]

Water and Wine

Sometime around ten or eleven in the morning, a servant with a trumpet appeared before the lord and his companions to *corner l'aiue*—literally "blow the water," in other words, to call them to dinner.

The water referred to was, presumably, that which the nobles used to wash their hands before dining. It certainly did not refer to drinking water, which was generally shunned. Despite the advice of the best physicians, who claimed that drinking water at mealtimes was good for the digestion, the nobles' beverage of choice was, overwhelmingly, wine. The quantities they drank were astonishing, especially in Britain. "Yet we must forgive the English," wrote a Franciscan monk, "if they are glad to drink wine when they can, for they have but little wine in their own country."[38]

Like feudalism and the jury system, the majority of wine was imported from France. Some 3 million gallons of wine were imported per year—a third of England's entire import trade! Some wines were better than others. As a clerk at Henry II's court wrote, "I have sometimes seen even great lords served with wine so muddy that a man must needs close his eyes and clench his teeth, wry-mouthed and shuddering, and filtering the stuff rather than drinking."[39]

Appeal by Arms

If a knight was charged with a felony and was not satisfied with the decision handed down by his lord or his peers, he might demand the right to defend himself "by his body," that is, by challenging his accuser to a duel. G. G. Coulton's anthology *Life in the Middle Ages,* includes a passage from a thirteenth-century law book that stipulates how such a trial by combat should be conducted.

"[The accuser and accused should both be] armed without iron and without the slightest armour, their heads uncovered, their hands and feet bare, with two staves tipped with horn of equal length, and each of them a target [shield] of four corners, without any other arms, whereby either of them may annoy the other. . . . If the defendant can defend himself until the stars can be seen in the firmament . . . our will is, that judgment pass for the defendant. . . . If the defendant be vanquished, let the judgment be this, that he be drawn and hanged, or put to such other painful death as we shall direct . . . and let the accuser . . . receive from us a notable reward."

In *Daily Living in the Twelfth Century,* Urban Tigner Holmes Jr. discusses how

women, as well as low-ranking men, used this right. "Women could have recourse to trial by combat. In that event they were permitted to find any champion who could be persuaded to fight for them. The theory back of these trials was that Divine punishment would be meted out to the perjurer [liar]. . . . Men of lower rank were allowed to have trial by combat, making use of cudgels [clubs], with or without a shield."

Women and commoners also had the option of undergoing trial by ordeal. For noblewomen, this usually meant being required to grasp a hot bar of iron, as Holmes explains.

"They walked with this in the bare hand before many witnesses. If the burn healed in a specific length of time, the defendant was adjudged innocent. A serf who was accused was usually given the ordeal of water. A huge cask was filled and a wooden board was set across the top. The victim undergoing the test was bound with a rope attached to his shoulders. If innocent he was supposed to sink; if guilty he would float."

A Social Occasion

Dinner was the main meal of the day and was served at midday in the big hall where court had been convened earlier. Like the holding of court, it was very much a social occasion. "It is not seemly that a lord should eat alone,"[40] counseled a thirteenth-century writer. In fact, if a vassal or a servant took his meals alone, instead of in the hall with his peers, it was considered extremely rude, even dangerous behavior. Like chapel attendance, communal meals were a way of creating a feeling of solidarity among the household, and solitary dining was believed to foster disorder.

Both the upper and the lower tables were spread with linen tablecloths. The food was distributed in bowls of wood or, in wealthier households, of silver. Each bowl was shared by two diners, who scooped out their individual portions onto thick slices of dry bread called trenchers. If soup or some other mostly liquid dish was served, spoons of silver or earthenware were handed out. Otherwise, the only eating utensils were the guests' fingers and the knives they carried at their belts.

After dinner the servants collected all the leftover food, including the grease- and gravy-soaked bread trenchers, in a basket and distributed it to the needy.

Bread and Meat

The two staples of the medieval diet were bread and meat, and there was a wide variety of each. The finest white bread was called *wastel*. *Simnel* was a sort of biscuit. *Treet* bread was made of unbolted flour, which meant the bran had not been sifted out. Com-

At dinnertime the castle's entire household met in the main hall to dine and socialize, including the lowliest servant and the lord himself.

mon wheat bread was even coarser, consisting mainly of what was left over from making the finer grades.

Ordinarily nobles would settle for nothing less than *wastel*, the top of the line; they even fed it to their dogs. Meanwhile, the common people often had to be content with loaves made of oats, rye, or barley.

In spite of a widely held notion that pork promoted leprosy, it was probably the most common meat on the castle table, followed closely by beef and mutton (sheep). In the warm months, meat was cooked, usually by roasting, soon after the animal was killed. But for meat to last all winter, it had to be salted; boiling was the usual method of preparing salt meat.

All sorts of birds were considered good eating, even swans and crows. In pious households, Wednesdays, Fridays, and Saturdays, as well as the whole Lenten period from Ash Wednesday to Easter, were considered fast days. On these days, the usual meat dishes were replaced by fish. Though castles with fish ponds could put some fresh catches on the table, other households relied mainly on salted herring, which quickly grew distasteful. A medieval schoolboy complained, "Thou wyll not beleve how wery I am off fyshe, and how moch I desir that flesh [meat] were cum in ageyn [again], for I have ate non other but salt fysh this Lent, and it hath engendyrde [engendered] so moch flewme [phlegm] within me that it stoppith my pyps [pipes] that I can unneth [neither] speke nother brethe."[41]

A less substantial meal, called supper, was served at dusk, usually between four and six in the evening. The emphasis at supper tended to be more on drink than on food. Well-to-do barons sometimes indulged in a late evening meal called a "rere supper," but moralists condemned this practice as leading to gluttony and lechery.

Generous to a Fault

One of the prime qualities a great lord was expected to display was generosity, or largesse. In *Daily Life in the Middle Ages*, Clara and Richard Winston explain that, according to the medieval way of thinking, "from largesse all other good qualities came, even courage. . . . Largesse to the Church, largesse to fellow noblemen, to guests, to servitors, to family—the upper-class man was required to behave as if his riches were inexhaustible."

Many nobles spent themselves into ruin in an attempt to demonstrate their generosity. The motives behind largesse were not always unselfish, of course. It was also a way of boasting that one had so much wealth he could give large amounts of it away—or even destroy it. One knight had a plot of ground plowed up and sown with silver coins. Another had thirty horses from his stable burned alive, just to show that he could afford to lose them.

Hunting and Hawking

Though meals often occupied several hours, a noble who was enjoying a period of peace—or, more likely, not enjoying it very much—was left with a good deal of leisure time. Thus, visitors were a welcome diversion. In fact, occasionally some bored baron might go so far as to deliberately reroute a well-traveled road so that it led travelers close to his castle, where he could invite them to stay a while. For men who were brought up considering warfare the ideal pastime, however, polite conversation did not furnish a very satisfactory substitute. They preferred active outdoor pursuits: riding, hunting, and hawking.

Lifestyles of the Rich and Noble

Noble hunters supervise as their attendants skin a freshly killed deer. Such lords seldom hunted out of necessity; most aristocratic hunters enjoyed the warlike aspect of hunting and the camaraderie between the participants, particularly in times of peace.

The hunter's favorite quarry was the deer. Hunting could be a way of providing fresh meat for the table, of course, but some nobles developed such a passion for the chase and the kill that they did in far more animals than they could possibly eat. In 1252 Richard of Cornwall and his companions bagged thirty-two bucks in the forest of Rockingham in the space of only nine days.

Sometime around 1260, a priest named Thomas of Chantimpré preached a cautionary tale about a knight whose appetite for hunting led him to

compel many of his tenants daily to wander and spend their labour in hunting with him; whereby very many left their own business of tilling the fields, and fell with their wives and children into poverty and want. It befel therefore one day that he went into the forest to chase the stag. . . . But when he had ridden all day in vain, and still saw the stag fleeing ever before his face, then his mind was turned to madness, and he pursued after him all night long with his whole train; so from that day forward no man ever saw or knew what had become of them or whither they were gone. Some said . . . that the earth opened up her jaws . . . and sucked them down to hell.[42]

Hawking—using birds of prey to hunt small animals—became an obsession with many nobles, too. They prided themselves on knowing all the jargon, or slang, of the sport and, according to Barbara W. Tuchman, "carried a favorite falcon, hooded, on the wrist wherever they went, indoors or out—to church,

to the assizes [judicial sessions], to meals. On occasion, huge pastries were served from which live birds were released to be caught by hawks unleashed in the banquet hall."[43]

"Never Give Up War!"

Other favorite sports included wrestling, cockfighting, and bullbaiting, in which a captive bull was set upon by dogs. Another brutish and brutal amusement involved two or more blindfolded men with clubs who chased a goose or a pig around an enclosure, trying to club it to death and usually succeeding instead in knocking one another senseless.

There were more subdued entertainments, of course, such as chess and gambling with dice, but they could be hazardous, too. The church condemned games of chance involving dice,

A philosopher (right) teaches a king to play chess, a popular and respectable entertainment during the Middle Ages.

not because they were inherently sinful, but because they encouraged wholesale cursing.

Dice players often had ample reason to curse. One young squire, coaxed into betting on a game at a tavern, lost all his money, his horse, his armor—everything, in fact, except the shirt on his back—before he was rescued by a friend. Dice games earned such a low reputation that a law passed in 1256 in France proclaimed, "Dice shall not be made in this dominion, and those using them shall be looked upon as suspicious characters."[44]

The game of chess, which was not as complex as it is today, was considered more respectable. An Italian bishop felt that "dice and chess were entirely different things: the first sinful; the second a most honorable exercise for Christians."[45] But in the heat of competition, chess was known to turn into a contact sport. The chess board was larger than those in use today and so were the pieces; thus, comments historian Holmes "if thrown with effective aim, they could inflict some damage. . . . Reinald Fitz Aymon killed in this way the knight who was playing with him . . . thereby starting a feud. This was a common source of feuds in the *chansons de geste* [epic poems]."[46]

Inevitably, no matter how many games he played, how many visitors he entertained, or how ardently he hunted and hawked, the typical knight or baron grew bored with castle life. He regarded these pursuits as merely a way of marking time until he could once again fulfill his true function in life: riding off to battle.

Bertrand de Born, a twelfth-century troubadour, or storyteller, of noble birth, spoke for his fellow nobles when he wrote:

I tell you I have no such joy as when I hear the shout

"On! On!" from both sides and the neighing of riderless steeds,

And groans of "Help me! Help me!"

And when I see both great and small

Fall in the ditches and on the grass

And see the dead transfixed by spear shafts!

Lords, mortgage your domains, castles, cities,

But never give up war![47]

The Lives of Women and Children

When the lord of a castle rode off to war, someone had to take care of business for him. The person in charge might be a steward—usually another nobleman of lower rank—but more often the responsibility fell to the lord's wife. Whether she was a duchess, a baroness, or a knight's lady, she was called the châtelaine.

Some châtelaines did far more than just oversee the daily routine of the castle. When the castle of Cesena in northern Italy was attacked during the lord's absence, châtelaine Marcia Ordelaffi doggedly directed its defense. According to historian Barbara W. Tuchman, the lady "refused all offers to negotiate despite repeated assaults, mining of walls, bombardment day and night by stones cast from siege engines, and the pleas of her father to surrender. Suspecting her councillor of secretly arranging a surrender, she had him arrested and beheaded."[48] Only when her knights threatened to desert did she negotiate and then did it so skillfully that she obtained safe conduct for everyone in the castle.

A Difficult Part to Play

Ordinarily the lady of the castle did not have to perform such aggressive duties. But, even when her husband was on the premises, she did play a substantial part in running the household.

Hers was a difficult part to play. On the one hand, she was expected to be subservient to the lord of the house and to obey his every wish. Women who disputed this fact of life risked being beaten by their husbands or even imprisoned, like the wife of French nobleman Gautier of Salins (she later escaped). On the other hand, she was expected to be the lord's partner, with a multitude of responsibilities of her own. She was in charge of the other women in the household and the young children as well. She oversaw the purchasing and distribution of supplies and made sure that the domestic servants did their jobs properly. Cloth was woven and made into clothing under her supervision; she might even do some of the weaving and sewing herself. Another of her duties was to entertain visitors to the castle and to ensure that they were received, to quote a twelfth-century writer, "quickly, courteously, and with good cheer."[49]

A woman might bring much more to a marriage, though, than just the ability to manage domestic affairs. Often the wife's dowry—the money and lands given to her by her father—was the source of much or most of her husband's wealth and status.

Women in a Man's World

The châtelaine's life was made even more difficult by the fact that she was one of only a few women in what was essentially a man's world. Ordinarily the only women to be found in a castle, besides the lord's wife, were a few ladies-in-waiting and perhaps several nursery servants.

With her behavior always under scrutiny, it was hard for a noblewoman to know how to conduct herself. According to Robert of Blois, a thirteenth-century French poet, "If she speaks, someone says it is too much. If she is silent, she is reproached for not knowing how to greet people. If she is friendly and courteous, someone pretends it is for love. If on the other hand she does not put on a bright face, she passes for being too proud."[50]

Though generosity was considered a virtue in the lord of the castle, it did not do for the lady to be too free in dispensing money or gifts. According to the author of *Les quatre ages de l'homme*, "If the wife and husband are both generous, it is the ruin of the house, while a wife's greater generosity shames her lord."[51]

Much importance was placed on a lady's appearance, but if she tried to improve it by powdering her face, dabbing her cheeks with vermilion, or applying a beauty mask made of mashed beans and mare's milk, the church chastised her. It also frowned upon women who dyed their hair or augmented it with false hair.

A châtelaine's many responsibilities included overseeing the weaving of cloth and the making of clothing, in which she herself might also participate.

Dressing the Part

Though the châtelaine was expected to dress elegantly, befitting her station, she was also liable to be accused of vanity by such critics as Franciscan monk Berthold von Regensburg:

> Ye will spend a good six months' work on a single veil, which is sinful great travail,—and all that men may praise thy dress. . . . And when thou shouldest be busy in the house with something needful for the goodman . . . or thy children, or thy guests, then art thou busy instead with thy hair or thy wimple [head covering]! . . . Ye men might put an end to this. . . . Take courage, and pluck up heart and tear it from her head, even though four or ten hairs should come away with it, and cast it into the fire![52]

Aside from such accessories as a veil or a wimple, women wore basically the same garments as men—with one notable exception. Despite a wealth of medieval jokes about who wore the pants in the family, a lady never wore *braies*. For modesty's sake, her linen *chainse*, instead of being ankle-length, hung all the way to her feet. Her surcoat was longer than a man's, too, and the sleeves were fuller. Often the fabric of the sleeves draped to the ground and had to be knotted up to keep them from dragging on the floor.

Practically Prisoners

Like the lord, the châtelaine had attendants who helped her dress and kept her company. These ladies-in-waiting were not mere servants; they were noble ladies of a lower social standing or the daughters of relatives sent to the castle to receive an education.

While strolling along the ramparts of a castle, medieval ladies display the height of fashion—embellished wimples and floor-length gowns.

From the older ladies, the young girls learned the social graces and the arts of sewing, embroidery, weaving, singing, and dancing plus some knowledge of first aid and healing herbs. Under the tutelage of the chaplain, or perhaps a clerk, they might also learn to do basic mathematics and pick up a smattering of other languages, including Latin. In some households, girls were even taught to ride, hunt, and hawk.

In others, the small contingent of women were practically prisoners. They were sequestered in separate quarters away from the men, and were closely guarded and given no opportunity to do much of anything except dress up and play games. One cleric at the time denounced such enforced idleness; placing himself in a woman's situation, he complained, "I do no other work but read my psalter [prayer book], work in gold or silk, hear the story of Thebes or Troy, play tunes on my harp, checkmate someone at chess, or feed the hawk on my wrist."[53]

Blindman's Buff, Ragman's Roll

In addition to chess, young ladies amused themselves playing *merels,* a sort of elaborate ticktacktoe game; tables, a board game similar to backgammon; and draughts or dames, which were much like checkers except that the pieces were square.

When guests came, everyone might engage in a rousing round of ragman's roll. In this game, humorous and sometimes crude verses were written on slips of paper and rolled up. Then each player drew a roll and read the verse, which was supposed to reveal something about the player's character. Other favorites were blindman's buff and hot cockles. In the latter, a blindfolded victim was slapped on the hands by one of the other players and had to guess who did the hitting.

Because books were so rare, reading was not a major pastime. But storytellers, both local ones and traveling professionals, were welcomed eagerly at the castle. So were musicians and minstrels of all kinds, from dignified harpers and troubadours who sang of heroes and saints to foolish jesters who did acrobatics and told off-color jokes.

Two or Three Tongues

Communication in the Middle Ages was not always easy, especially between the different orders of society. Most countries in Europe had at least two official languages, as Marc Bloch points out in *Feudal Society.*

"On the one hand there was the immense majority of uneducated people, each one imprisoned in his regional dialect. . . . On the other hand, there was the little handful of educated people who, constantly alternating between the local everyday speech and the universal language of learning [Latin], were in the true sense bilingual."

The countries conquered by the Normans had to cope with a third tongue. The English language had reached a high state of development before the conquest, both in written and spoken form. But by the end of the twelfth century, French had become the language of the upper classes in England. The typical noble knew only a smattering of English and must have been totally bewildered when trying to converse with a Scot or a Welshman.

Dancing was another popular form of entertainment, even though it was condemned by the church. Etienne de Bourbon, a thirteenth-century friar, preached that "the devil is the inventor and governor and disposer of dances and dancers."[54] Yet his colleague Thomas of Chantimpré grudgingly admitted that "those dances which are held at the weddings of the faithful may be partly, though not wholly, excused; since it is right for those folk thus to have the consolation of a moderate joy, who have joined together in the laborious life of matrimony."[55] In an effort to discourage dancing, another priest solemnly told the probably fictional tale of a count who allowed so much dancing that the floor of his great hall weakened and collapsed, throwing the revelers, including the count's own daughter, to their deaths.

Other Entertainments

During religious festivals the ladies delighted in watching, and sometimes participating in, mystery plays depicting stories from the Bible. These plays were sponsored by the local church and enacted by its parishoners. An elaborate mystery play performed at Bourges, France, lasted forty days and featured nearly five hundred actors, who were so convincing that, according to one witness, "the greater part of the spectators judged it to be real and not feigned."[56]

Of course, few mystery plays were this ambitious. But most tried to liven up the proceedings by featuring special effects such as

A mystery play is enacted during a religious festival, drawing throngs of spectators. Medieval ladies sometimes participated in such dramas.

Jesus being lifted into the clouds (by weights and pulleys), Noah's flood (casks of water poured over the stage), and bloody tortures and beheadings (using the blood of a sheep or an ox). In one production a fake donkey brought howls of laughter from the audience when it lifted its tail and dropped fake donkey dung onto the stage.

In good weather there were outdoor games such as tennis, in which the stuffed leather ball was struck not with a racket but with the open hand; a cross between billiards and croquet, played with wooden balls and a mallet; and a game that resembled bowling except that the players knocked down the pins by throwing a stick.

The Game of Love

Often the gentlemen of the castle were invited to join in these games. But, overall, contact between the lord's men and the châtelaine's ladies was limited. The lord, after all, was responsible for the care and protection of the women and girls in his household, and he preferred that they avoid any romantic entanglements that might prove embarrassing. Though sexual encounters certainly occurred, for the most part the men were forced to admire the ladies from afar.

As a result, in the same way that rough-and-tumble games provided a sort of substitute for actual warfare, a substitute for physical love developed in the form of *courtoisie,* or courtly love. It was an elaborate code of manners that demanded that the loved one be idealized, figuratively placing her on a pedestal. According to the rules of *courtoisie,* the lover's passion was expected to be spiritual and pure. The beloved was really more of a mother figure than an object of desire, and her admirer adored her in an almost childlike way.

"A Rather Remote Figure"

It is hardly surprising that grown men should long so for a mother figure. As a child, the typical nobleman had precious little contact with his real mother. Historian Margaret Wade Labarge describes the fate of most medieval upper-class children:

> Almost immediately after birth, they were handed over to the care of a nurse whose duties . . . included not only the physical care of the child, but also the display of affection which is now considered essentially maternal. . . . She was ordered to nourish and feed the child . . . and comfort it if it wept. . . . The mother must have been a rather remote figure.[57]

Many mothers did not even breastfeed their babies, but handed the duty over to a wet nurse, a commoner who was pregnant or had recently given birth herself. By the thirteenth century, the use of wet nurses had become so widespread that manuals for parish priests advised them to oppose the practice, since both the Bible and the medical community considered it contrary to nature.

The use of a wet nurse was hardly a universal practice, though. Some noblewomen relished the bond that nursing created with their children. A French poet tells of a woman who objected to wet nurses on the grounds that a commoner's milk might contaminate her son's noble blood. One day, when she left the boy with an attendant, he

> wailed sore and howled; wherefore the maiden called a damosel and bade her suckle the child. . . . When the Countess heard this . . . she flew, all trembling with rage, and caught her child under the arms . . . rolled him and caught him by the

A medieval drawing depicts the typical attire of thirteenth-century nurse-servants, who were responsible for caring for the lord and lady's children.

shoulders, that he delayed not to give up [vomit] the milk which he had sucked. Yet ever after were his deeds and renown the less, even to the day of his death.[58]

The father's role in the rearing of children was mainly to discipline them, and the discipline was often harsh. According to the prevailing attitude in the Middle Ages, parents who were too lenient or affectionate encouraged bad behavior in their children. As thirteenth-century commentator Philip of Novara wrote, "Few children perish from excess of severity but many from being permitted too much."[59]

Affection and Amusement

Medieval children were not entirely deprived of parental affection, though. A chronicler of the time described a game of hide-and-seek in which the mother conceals herself from the child "and lets him sit alone and look anxiously around and call 'Dame, dame!' and weep a while, and then she leapeth forth lightly with outspread arms and embraceth and kisseth him, and wipeth his eyes." The same manuscript also shows that fathers comforted their children in much the same way they do today: "If a child stumble against anything or hurt himself men beat the thing that he hurteth himself upon, and the child is well pleased, and forgetteth all his hurt, and stoppeth his tears."[60]

The children of the nobility had no shortage of amusements. The toys they played with were, for the most part, the same ones that would delight children for the next five hundred years: dolls, toy soldiers, miniature vehicles, and animals. A favorite plaything for boys was a pair of wooden knights that could be made to engage in a pretend jousting match. Older boys faced off against one another with "swords" made of the dry, woody stem of the plantain.

In addition to the hunting dogs and hawks and horses, most households kept animals of various kinds as pets. Cats were valued more for their mousing abilities than as companions, but dogs commonly shared the dining room and bedroom with the family. So did pet birds—parrots, magpies, and ravens. Occasionally a castle had a more unusual pet such as a tame monkey, badger, or weasel.

Learning Lessons

Many nobles, especially those who emphasized the military role of their class, considered any education beyond the ability to write one's name a waste of time. Though nearly every important church maintained a school, these were meant mainly for children who were training to be members of the clergy.

But a fair number of knights and barons realized the value of learning how to read, write, and figure. Some enrolled their sons in church schools; others provided tutors for them at home—and sometimes for their daughters as well. Usually the lessons being taught were pretty basic, as historian Jay Williams explains:

> Most began with the ABC's, learned from a hornbook. This was a piece of parchment on which were written the letters of the alphabet and perhaps the Lord's Prayer, the whole covered over with a piece of transparent horn. In addition, pupils were taught to sing some Latin hymns and to read the books of Psalms in Latin. As they grew a little older, they might be taught to read and write in their own language. . . . A little arithmetic was sometimes taught, but this was considered a difficult subject.[61]

A good education consisted of more than just academic subjects. It stressed moral and social lessons as well. Courtesy books, which gave instructions on proper behavior, were also popular. One such book advises that

> The good child should stand erect
>
> Before his lord to eat.
>
> He should not lean against things
>
> Nor scratch any of his limbs . . .
>
> If someone gives you a gift, small or great . . .
>
> Kneel down to accept it
>
> And sweetly tell him thanks.[62]

"The Rigor of the Rule"

In his autobiography, written around 1115, a French abbot named Guibert recalled how he began his education at the age of six in "the dining hall of our house." The tutor, he wrote, "loved me as well as he did himself." Unfortunately, he was apparently not a very capable teacher, for he showered Guibert "with a hail of blows and harsh words while he was forcing me to learn what he could not teach." Though Guibert was eager to learn, he felt left out when he saw that other children "wandered everywhere at will and were unchecked in the indulgence of such inclinations as were natural at their age."[63]

Beatings at the hands of teachers and tutors were routine, and students of the time were mostly resigned to the fact—but not always. When a professor at Malmesbury Abbey in Wiltshire, England, grew too abusive, his pupils rebelled and stabbed him to death with their pens.

Not all educators were so unenlightened. A few, such as the abbot of Bec, France, recognized the need for "kindness, compassion, cheerful encouragement, loving forbearance, and much else of the same kind." One school

In medieval schools young nobles received basic educations, primarily mastering reading and writing while also learning moral and social lessons.

even scheduled regular recess periods for students, "lest they should be exhausted by the rigor of the Rule without the interpolation of recreation."[64]

Sent Elsewhere

The greater part of the typical noble child's education took place not in his own household but in a relative's. At around the age of seven, most boys and girls were sent elsewhere to be educated, typically to the castle of an aunt or an uncle. The girls spent their time with the lady of the castle; the boys served as valets, or pages, learning to wait on tables and do other household chores.

When girls reached their early teen years, they were considered ready to marry and start a household of their own. Though most marriages were arranged by the parents, the church insisted that certain rules be observed: the bride should be at least fifteen, she should not be closely related to the groom, and she must give her "free consent."

Boys were also considered adults in their teens, but most did not marry until they became knights, and that required a long apprenticeship. They went on performing the duties of a page for seven years or so—and those seven years could seem extremely long, for life as a lowly page could be trying. Götz von Berlichingen, a medieval German knight, recalls in his autobiography,

I was brought up as a page in the house of the Markgraf [count]; on whom . . . I must needs wait at table. Now it befel upon a time that I sat at meat beside a Pole, who had waxed his hair with eggs. . . . When I sprang up from my place . . . I ruffled his fine hair. . . . He thrust at me with a bread-

knife, but missed me. . . . I had both a long and a short blade at my side, yet I drew but the short one, and smote him therewith about the pate [head].

The Iron Hand

Götz von Berlichingen, the impulsive German page who was imprisoned for quarreling with a guest, grew up to be an equally fearless knight. He acquired the nickname "Götz of the Iron Hand" after he lost his right hand at the siege of Landshut. An excerpt from Berlichingen's autobiography, reprinted in G. G. Coulton's *Life in the Middle Ages,* relates the ordeal.

"[A cannon ball] shot in two my swordhilt, so that the one half entered right into my arm, and three armplates therewithal . . . and these, I believe, tore off my hand betwixt the gauntlet [steel glove] and the armpiece; my arm was shattered behind and before. . . . I made as though nothing had befallen me, turned my horse softly round, and, in spite of all, came back to my own folk without let or hindrance from the enemy. . . . I was spoiled now for a fighting man. Yet then I bethought me of a man at arms . . . who also had but one hand, notwithstanding which he could do his devoir [duty] against his foe in the field as well as any other man. . . . Therefore, thought I, might I but get me some little help by means of an iron hand, then I would prove myself as doughty [courageous] in the field, in spite of all, as any other maimed man. . . . [Now] for wellnigh sixty years I have waged wars, feuds, and quarrels with but one fist."

As punishment, the boy was imprisoned in the castle tower until his captain "set me free again . . . and spake in my behalf, and excused me."[65]

Though it is obvious from this account that pages were not exactly ignorant about how to handle weapons, their military training did not begin officially until they reached puberty. "When their voices started to change," writes Urban Tigner Holmes Jr., "or perhaps even earlier as they showed manly strength, they were sent downstairs to the lord himself."[66] There they would learn the skills they needed to pursue the noble's true calling—warfare.

A Soldier's Life

There does not seem to have been any formal ceremony that marked a boy's passage from page to squire, or knight-in-training. Often there was not even a clear boundary between the two roles. Well before they reached their teens, most boys had begun honing their knightly skills—practicing with weapons, riding and caring for horses, and learning how to hunt and hawk. But when they made the transition from page to squire, these things became their primary occupation.

The Lance and the Sword

Because the knight was, above all, a mounted warrior, the most important weapon was the lance. Much of the squire's time was spent learning how to properly use the weapon. Around the time of the conquest of England, the lance seems to have been rather short—probably ten feet at the longest—and light, designed to be thrown like a javelin. Later on it developed into something much longer and heftier, as military scholar Michael Prestwich explains:

> The length was probably about fourteen feet; the weapon was carried vertically until lowered for the charge. The lance depended for its effect on the combined momentum of horse and rider; it was therefore of little use after the initial

shock of impact. Lances were easily broken, and were of little value in a mêlée [hand-to-hand fighting].[67]

The ability to wield a fourteen-foot pole effectively required a lot of practice. Mounted on horseback, or perhaps on a wooden "horse" with wheels, squires made pass after pass at a metal ring suspended from a wooden arm, trying to catch the ring on the tip of the lance. An even more tricky device called a quintain resembled a human figure with a club in one hand. Unless a rider hit the figure squarely in the chest with his lance, the quintain pivoted around and clobbered him with the club.

The other essential weapon was, of course, the sword. Though boys often began practicing with a light fencing foil at an early age, that sport bore little resemblance to the art of fighting with a broadsword.

In the twelfth and thirteenth centuries, when chain mail was the soldier's primary protection, the typical battle sword had a flat blade three inches wide at the hilt and three feet long, designed for cutting rather than thrusting. As heavier plate armor came into use, swords became lighter and more pointed, suitable for thrusting between the joints of the armor. An alternative was the massive two-handed sword, which could do much damage through sheer momentum.

Learning how to handle a sword took plenty of practice, too, and a good deal of strength. Squires spent endless hours hacking at a wooden post with a rebated, or dulled, sword. To give them a chance to try their skills on a real opponent, they were given either cudgels (clubs) or six-foot-long quarterstaves and were paired off against one another.

Archery might also be on the agenda, though in France most nobles regarded the bow as strictly a commoner's weapon, and an unsporting one at that.

In addition to his military training, a squire was ordinarily expected to perform specific household duties, as Jay Williams explains:

> His chief task might be waiting at table, or managing his master's great warhorse and breaking in new mounts. The body squire . . . was the personal attendant of a lord, and there might be more than one. They carried their master's lance, shield, or helmet, looked after his personal belongings, and armed him. . . . They then followed him into battle or the tournament, although, until they were made *armigers* [knights] they were not allowed to fight.[68]

In the heat of tournament or battle, however, young men who had spent the last several years being trained to fight were likely to forget or to disregard this rule.

Becoming a Knight

Theoretically a squire could be dubbed—declared a knight—by any other knight, however ordinary. But the higher the rank of the

A chivalrous Norman knight prepares to lob a short lance, which was often thrown like a javelin at its target.

nobleman who conveyed the honor, the greater the glory, so most young men preferred to be knighted by the lord himself or, better yet, by his lord's lord.

Early in the Middle Ages, dubbing was a fairly simple matter. The candidate for knighthood knelt before his lord, who delivered the *colée*, a blow of the hand or of the flat of a sword blade on the head or shoulders. Then the new knight's sword, sometimes blessed by a priest, was strapped to his waist. Occasionally the knighting occurred on the battlefield as a reward for exceptional valor.

By the end of the twelfth century, however, becoming a knight usually involved an elaborate Christian ceremony. First the candidate was bathed, symbolically washing away his sins. Then he donned a white robe that symbolized his pledge to defend God's law. Often the knighting took place on the eve of a battle; but, if time allowed, the candidate performed a vigil, standing or kneeling before the altar of the church or chapel all night long. In the morning he was presented with his spurs and his sword, completing the ceremony.

Noble birth was not necessarily a prerequisite for becoming a knight, at least not in England. A common soldier who showed extraordinary bravery or devotion might be rewarded with knighthood. It was not rare to find a knight whose parents were peasants or serfs.

While a squire dressed in a white robe kneels on a pillow, an armor-clad lord dubs him a knight, ceremoniously honoring the squire for his wartime heroics.

An Expensive Undertaking

By the same token, not all young men of the nobility chose to become knights. Knighthood was an expensive undertaking. In order to own a warhorse and all the requisite armor and weapons, a knight either had to be fairly well off or had to have his equipment furnished by someone wealthy.

The warhorse—also called a charger or *destrier*—was, writes Michael Prestwich, "the most expensive possession of a knight. . . . It was a highly trained, expertly bred beast, capable of carrying an impressive load of man and armour in the terrifying conditions of battle. Mares were not used for this task; the spirit and aggression of a stallion were considered essential."[69]

In the twelfth century a top-quality charger might set a knight back only two to six pounds—about five times the price of a good cow. By the end of the thirteenth century, he could expect to pay over ten pounds for one, and perhaps as much as sixty pounds. Most knights, remember, earned less than one hundred pounds a year from their estates, and some earned far less.

In addition to the warhorse, a knight needed a palfrey, or ordinary saddle horse, suitable for riding long distances. When a horse became sick, lame, or exhausted, a fresh mount had to be ready for him. In the thirteenth century a palfrey cost in the neighborhood of 60 to 120 shillings (3 to 6 pounds).

The plate armor so often associated with knights did not come into general use until the end of the thirteenth century. Prior to that time armor consisted primarily of a long mail shirt, or hauberk, that was sometimes paired with *chausses*, or leggings, made of mail—that is, row on row of interlocking steel rings, sometimes one layer, sometimes two or three.

The accoutrements of knighthood, including the hauberk and chausses *worn by this twelfth-century knight, were incredibly costly.*

Hand-Me-Down Hauberks

Because armor was such a big investment and so time-consuming to make, when a knight retired from service he customarily passed his armor on to a younger friend or relative. In her book *A Baronial Household of the Thirteenth Century,* Margaret Wade Labarge elaborates on this tradition as well as on the maintenance of the valuable armor.

"When Bartholomew de Legh died around 1230, he left . . . a hauberk and mailed shoes to the earl of Winchester . . . while his nephew got a hauberk, mail stockings, and a mail covering—perhaps for the horse—all

of which Bartholomew himself had earlier inherited from his brother. Although capable of lasting for long periods, chain mail was particularly liable to rust. . . . At the earl of Cornwall's castle of Wallingford, two men were paid 6s [shillings] for polishing the arms twice a year; seven bushels of bran were bought for polishing, and also for storing the arms. Another method employed for cleaning chain mail was to put it in a barrel or leather bag with sand and vinegar, then the container was rolled and shaken to remove the rust. Such cleaning was absolutely necessary to prevent the armour's rapid decay."

A well-constructed hauberk might weigh as little as twenty pounds, but most weighed twice or even three times that much. It was quite a burden for the average man, who was not very large by today's standards. A man who stood five feet ten was considered tall; a short fellow might be only five feet two.

Armor did not come cheap, either. At the end of the twelfth century a hauberk could cost over a pound; by the middle of the thirteenth century, it was more likely to cost six or seven pounds. In addition, most knights wore a padded tunic, or *gambeson,* under the hauberk and a cloth surcoat over it and, of course, a helmet—usually a pot-shaped steel cap with a nasal, a bar that protected the face. Add to all this the price of a sword and shield and the cost of keeping it all in good repair.

A knight might also have to cope with the expense of maintaining a household; and, if taken prisoner, he would likely have to pay a sizable ransom to obtain his freedom. All in all, knighthood constituted a considerable financial responsibility, one that many young

men, especially those who were not in line to inherit lands or money from their fathers and had no prospect of marrying a rich woman, were unable or unwilling to assume. "As a squire," writes Frances Gies, "a man had a good chance of having his needs taken care of, his horse and equipment furnished. As a knight, he would be expected to furnish himself with not one but three horses and in addition to equip his own squire, with the total cost running into hundreds of pounds."[70] It is no wonder that many boys of noble birth chose to put off becoming knights well into manhood or sometimes all their lives.

Making Ends Meet

Those who did opt to be dubbed knights sometimes had to struggle to make ends meet. During wartime, knights could make a good living in two accepted ways: first, by taking their enemies prisoner and demanding a ransom for their release; second, by claiming the money and other valuables they found in the castles they captured.

The unwritten code of chivalry by which knights supposedly lived specified that they should not prey on members of the clergy, peasants, or merchants. But many knights took advantage of the breakdown of law and order that occurred in wartime to rob merchants and rich clergymen on the roads and to steal livestock from the farms of peasants. One troubadour of the period bemoaned this practice: "Oh, fie upon the knight who drives off sheep, robs churches and travelers."[71] But twelfth-century troubadour Bertrand de Born celebrated it: "We'll soon seize the usurer's [money lender's] gold; there won't be a packhorse on the roads; no burgher [townsman] will go without fear, nor any merchant heading for France. If you want to be rich, you have only to take!"[72]

By contrast, a prolonged period of peace could prove ruinous for knights of little means. It meant, writes Marc Bloch, "the disdainful indifference of the great, who would have no more need of them; the importunities [demands] of money-lenders; the heavy plough-horse instead of the mettlesome charger; iron spurs instead of gold—in short an economic crisis as well as a disastrous loss of prestige."[73]

Little Wars

What these knights needed was a peacetime pursuit that could bring them some measure of the glory and profit they got from engaging in war. They provided themselves with such a pursuit by staging a mock war, known as a tourney or tournament—also called "French combat" because it originated in France. The main difference between a tournament and a battle was that, in a tournament, the object was not to kill an opponent but to capture him. Nevertheless, a mock battle could be as brutal as the real thing.

Squires struggle to free their downed knight's foot from the saddle's stirrup during a brutal tournament mêlée.

Up until the middle of the thirteenth century, these "little wars" were basically just that: Two opposing sides engaged in a wild free-for-all called a mêlée that often resulted in wholesale injury or death. A number of the participants in a tournament held in 1257 were so badly battered that they never recovered. At another enormous mock battle that took place near Cologne, Germany, more than sixty knights were killed.

England's King Henry II, dismayed at seeing so many of his vassals wounded or killed, went so far as to prohibit the staging of tournaments. The church also strongly objected to what they called horse fairs and periodically banned them. As a Cistercian monk wrote in the mid–thirteenth century,

> Two mortal sins are committed at tournaments . . . pride because men joust [fight with lances on horseback] for the sake of earthly praise, and disobedience because it is done against the prohibition of the Holy Church; wherefore those who are slain in tournaments are buried apart from the faithful and without the churchyard.[74]

An Elaborate Spectacle

Despite the disapproval of their church and king, the nobility continued to hold tournaments, partly because they considered them a valuable training ground for soldiers. Roger de Hovedon, an English chronicler of the time, observed that

> a knight cannot shine in war if he has not prepared for it in tourneys. He must have seen his own blood flow, have had his teeth crackle under the blow of an opponent, have been dashed to earth . . . and

twenty times have leaped up again more set than ever upon the fight. Then he will be able to face actual war with the hope of victory.[75]

The organizers of tournaments did make some concessions to their critics, though, by making the contests less bloody and more strictly organized. Williams notes that

> codes of rules were adopted and different types of tournaments were introduced, such as the Round Table, in which contestants took the parts of King Arthur's knights . . . sprawling tournaments gave way to smaller ones held within a fenced-off ground, called the lists. These were easier to watch. A grandstand was built along one side for the noble spectators. . . . As time went on, the tournaments became an elaborate spectacle, almost more of a pageant than a contest of arms.[76]

In 1194, after the death of Henry II, tournaments again received royal approval in England. In 1316 the pope withdrew the church's ban on them, too; his reasoning was that they at least helped train soldiers to fight in the Crusades. Now that they were legal, tournaments became like modern-day sporting events and were carefully scheduled by the various lords who hosted them so that they were spread evenly throughout the year. Each host tried to entice the most accomplished knights to fight for him. The more successful a lord's "team" was, the greater his reputation.

Born to Fight

Young knights seeking to build reputations for themselves attended each of these tourneys.

Although the goal of a tournament was to gain fame by capturing rather than killing one's opponent, many knights were seriously injured during such contests.

Some of the older, more experienced ones became the medieval equivalent of professional athletes; they made a career out of defeating lesser knights at tournaments. The victor in a contest got to keep or sell off his opponent's horse and armor; he was even permitted to take the loser prisoner and demand a ransom.

Some of these knights-errant were amazingly successful at their trade. The renowned twelfth-century knight William the Marshal won twelve horses at a single tournament; in just one season of jousting, he and a companion held a total of three hundred fellow knights for ransom.

William was not always so lucky. At a tournament in France he captured a knight on horseback but, as he passed through town with the man in tow, the prisoner was knocked from the saddle by a low-hanging rain gutter. Oblivious, William went on to his tent and told his squire to take charge of the knight he had captured, leaving the young squire quite bewildered.

Ultimately, as with the other games nobles engaged in to pass the time, tournaments were no substitute for all-out war. "Gentle [noble] knights were born to fight," wrote French chronicler Jean Froissart in the

As the Middle Ages advanced, helmets and other armor grew ever bulkier and covered more of the knight's body and face until it became practically impossible to recognize who was inside.

The need to identify oneself and one's opponent led to the use of distinctive insignia, called coats of arms, on the knight's surcoat, shield, and banner. This developed into the art known as heraldry, as Michael Prestwich points out in *Armies and Warfare in the Middle Ages.*

"In the early stages, heraldic devices were only for the great men. . . . But heraldry soon multiplied; the need to identify men in tournaments being quite as important as the recognition of friends and enemies in battle. . . . Coats of arms came, however, to incorporate much more than that, being emblems of family pride and honour. . . . Men must have felt that one purpose in campaigning was to justify and further ennoble the arms that they bore. . . .

Important as heraldry was, with men taking much pride in their arms, it was nevertheless possible to discard them altogether, or to wear someone else's. Edward III frequently appeared incognito [unidentified] in tournaments, perhaps because no one would

fight properly against the king in his own name. . . . At Bannockburn the earl of Gloucester did not wear a surcoat bearing his coat of arms. This led to his death; had the Scots known who he was, they would not have killed him, such would have been his ransom."

Heraldic emblems, like the coat of arms on this rather simplistic shield, allowed knights to distinguish between friends and foes.

fourteenth century, "and war ennobles all who engage in it without fear or cowardice."[77]

"The Adventure of Life in Death"

Not all knights, though, accepted their role as warriors without reservations, for war meant

misery and deprivation as well as glory and profit. As another fourteenth-century writer observed,

Knights who are at the wars are forever swallowing their fear. They expose themselves to every peril; they give up their bodies to the adventure of life in death. . . . Today enough to eat, tomorrow nothing . . . a bad bed, poor sleep with their armor still on their backs, burdened with iron, the enemy an arrow-shot off. . . . Such is their calling.[78]

Small wonder that some knights preferred to pay a fee, called shield money or scutage, instead of serving their military obligation. Their lord then hired soldiers with the money to fight in place of his vassals.

A fourteenth-century poem, "The Vows of the Heron," gives a perceptive picture of the ambivalent attitude many fighting men surely had toward their profession:

> When we are in taverns, drinking strong wine, and ladies with white throats and tight bodices pass by and look at us . . . nature makes our hearts desire to fight, looking for mercy [romantic interest] from them as a result. . . . But when we are in the field, on our trotting warhorses, shields hung round our necks and lances lowered, a great frost numbing us, limbs crushed before and behind, and our enemies advancing on us, then we would like to be in a great cellar, and never make a vow again.[79]

A Member of the Garrison

One of the biggest drawbacks of being a professional soldier was the difficulty of maintaining a permanent home or supporting a family. As historian Christopher Hohler observes, "In time of war a knight could expect to be fighting away from home, and he was in no position to afford an elaborate kind of house or pay trained men to defend it. He might . . . find himself living in somebody else's castle as its hereditary castellan [overseer] or as a member of its hereditary garrison."[80]

In England, this hereditary garrison did not exist. But a knight was expected, as part of his military obligation, to spend several months each year, even in peacetime, as a member of his lord's castle guard. If he did not want to leave home, he could instead pay a fee similar to scutage.

French knights did this same sort of annual tour of duty, but French castles ordinarily had, in addition, a permanent corps of soldiers called, in Latin, the *milites gregarii*,

Medieval knights were obligated to spend part of each year serving in their lord's garrison. Here, a fifteenth-century knight rallies to stop the invasion of his lord's castle by enemy forces.

who, as Georges Duby explains, "spent their life together as members of their lord's entourage. . . . Life for these warriors was brutal and fiercely competitive; they slept together as a body in the castle hall . . . and their feelings toward their fellow-warriors were probably often ambivalent, veering sharply from love to hatred." It was not a position that other knights tended to covet, for, Duby continues, "if a castle fell into enemy hands, it was not unusual for the permanent garrison to be blinded or have their right hands [the sword hand] cut off if they were not all killed outright."[81]

CHAPTER

6 Life Among the Lowly

The upper-class contingent in a castle was not necessarily limited to just the lord and his corps of knights plus the châtelaine and her small group of companions. The retinue of even a minor baron could be quite sizable; a household of only twenty to twenty-five was considered small. Many lords, in fact, kept more servants than they really needed, in order to demonstrate how affluent they were.

A great lord's wealth and rank were measured, too, by the number of members of his household who were not commoners but fellow nobles of lesser rank. Some of these lesser nobles held offices of considerable responsibility. The most important was the steward, or seneschal, who was, to quote historian Kate Mertes, "in charge of discipline and order in the household, seeing that all runs smoothly—a kind of general manager."[82]

A steward (left) was often responsible for assigning work to the lord's villeins, or local peasants, as well as acting as the castle's general manager.

In a relatively small household, the steward might also serve as the treasurer. According to a thirteenth-century law book, "It is the steward's duty to account . . . for the expenses of the household, and to ascertain the total of the day's expenditures. . . . And all the serjeants [minor officials] are answerable . . . to the steward for their offices. And he is bound to bear witness to what they do."[83]

If there was a separate treasurer, or wardrober, he was also likely to be high born, as was the marshal who was in charge of the horses, the hawks, and the hounds, and the chamberlain, who controlled the budget for items that were not food-related.

"A Convenient, Honourable Living"

Positions of lesser importance were often filled by nobles, too. Mertes says that many lords "took their higher servants from among the families of their community of peers. . . . Household service provided a convenient, honourable living for landless younger sons of the upper ranks of society."[84]

At roughly the same social level as these minor nobles were the clergymen and clerks of the household. At the very least, every castle felt obliged to have a chaplain. The ideal chaplain, according to a Franciscan friar, should be "devoted to the divine sacraments, strenuous in the ecclesiastical offices, honest in manners, and circumspect [careful] in actions."[85]

Seeing to the spiritual needs of a noble household could be a trying task for a clergyman. Although religion was an integral part of everyday life in the Middle Ages, the average person was not particularly devout. One member of the clergy complained that, at mass, his flock were often "busying them-

selves with other things and paying no attention to the service nor saying their prayers."[86]

Communion and confession were supposed to be observed every Sunday and holy day, but in actuality few churchgoers managed them more than once or twice a year. Many knights did not even bother to attend mass. When one such soldier was reminded that regular attendance was important for the salvation of his soul, he replied, "This I knew not; nay, I thought the priests performed their mass for the offerings' sake"[87]—in order to collect money, in other words.

In a large household, the chaplain might have an assistant or two. In addition, there might be a cleric known as an almoner, who was in charge of collecting money, food, and cast-off clothing and distributing it to the sick and the needy. Most lords also retained one or more clerks to take care of accounts and correspondence.

Household Help

Even in the households of great nobles, however, most of the important servants came not from the ranks of the gentry but from yeoman or peasant families and ordinarily from the immediate vicinity of the castle.

Some of the positions held by commoners carried with them considerable responsibility. Often these jobs were hereditary, in practice at least, if not officially. A father trained his son, who eventually took over the position.

Most castle servants were men, and nearly all of them were unmarried. In fact, the lord usually actively discouraged his householders from marrying, feeling that it would undermine their loyalty to him. A man with a family seldom rose very far in rank, in any case, and his wife and children ordinarily

For the most part, the common people were resigned to their lot in life. But if the local lord demanded too much of them without giving anything in return, they might grow discontented enough to protest, even to rise up in revolt. In *A Distant Mirror,* Barbara W. Tuchman tells how, in 1358, the villagers of St. Leu in France revolted.

"[They] held an indignation meeting in the cemetery after vespers. They blamed the nobles for their miseries. . . . What were they good for except to oppress poor peasants? . . . Without further council and no arms but the staves and knives that some carried, a group of about 100 rushed in fierce assault upon the nearest manor, broke in, killed the knight, his wife, and children, and burned the place down. Then, according to [Jean] Froissart . . . 'they went to a strong castle, tied the knight to a stake while his wife and daughter were raped . . . then they killed the wife who was pregnant and afterward the daughter and all the children and lastly the knight and burned and destroyed the castle.'"

The peasants also burned and looted other estates; the uprising grew and spread to towns and cities before it was quelled by a force of mounted knights.

lived outside the castle. So did the two employees who traditionally were female: the laundress and the ale wife, who, as the name implies, was responsible for brewing all the ale consumed in the castle.

Since preparing food for a large household was a major task, the cook and the baker held essential positions. The baker, with the help of an assistant, kept a constant stream of loaves issuing from the giant oven, which was housed in a separate building in the bailey. The peasants in the vicinity were usually expected to bring their bread here to be baked, too—for a fee, of course.

Ordinarily grain was ground into flour for the bread at a water-powered mill near the castle. Though the lord owned the mill, it would most likely be run by a yeoman miller who paid rent for the privilege. The peasants who grew grain brought it there to be ground, too—again for a fee, usually a portion of the flour. Some castles had a smaller on-site mill, usually run by hand or by horsepower, so that during a siege the garrison could grind grain fresh rather than keeping a store of flour that would grow moldy and full of weevils.

The Castle Cook

The cook was aided in his work by a large staff—many of them boys from the surrounding area—and a rather limited array of kitchen utensils. There were no stoves, of course, so all the cooking was done in the vast fireplace of the cookhouse or, when a feast demanded larger quantities of food than usual, over an open fire outside in the bailey.

There was a spit in the fireplace where a whole deer or pig could be roasted and a hook-and-chain device on which a large cast iron cauldron could be raised or lowered. Smaller pots were equipped with legs so they could straddle the fire.

Considering the primitive equipment, the stifling heat that pervaded the cookhouse in the summer, and the unreliable nature of the help, it is not surprising that cooks had a reputation for being short-tempered and overbearing. They were known for the hard knocks they delivered to the boys who worked for them.

Though the medieval cook had few alternatives in terms of tools and cooking methods, he did have a wide range of choices when it came to spicing up the food. Some seasonings, such as mustard seed and parsley, could be grown right in the castle garden. Others, such as cloves and saffron, had to be imported at great expense. Such costly spices were kept under lock and key and issued to the cook in carefully regulated amounts—sometimes quite large amounts since the nobility of the time were inordinately fond of spicy dishes.

One astonishing recipe for preserves calls for—in addition to nuts, turnips, carrots, pumpkins, and peaches—large quantities of horseradish, cloves, cinnamon, pepper, ginger, nutmeg, saffron, red cedar, mustard seed, anise, fennel, coriander, and caraway!

Part-Time Physicians

Herbs and spices played an important role not only in cooking but also in medicine. Fennel, for example, supposedly was good for soothing stomach problems, increasing a mother's milk, and curing watery eyes and worms in the ears. Sugar was even prescribed by some as a remedy for chest ailments.

Much of the medicine that was practiced in the household was the responsibility of the châtelaine and her attendants. But the lord's barber was assumed to have some skill in extracting teeth, setting fractures, binding wounds, and letting blood—a regular monthly routine for many nobles, which was almost universally thought to promote good health.

A wealthy household might retain a full-time physician, but most had to summon a doctor from elsewhere when serious illness struck.

The Skilled and the Unskilled

Though the lord of a castle placed a lot of importance on eating well and on staying healthy, his top priority was being ready to wage war at the drop of a helmet. So the most valued member of his household may well have been the blacksmith. As historian William Stearns Davis writes,

> He has to keep a great quantity of weapons and armor in constant order; he has to do all the recurring small jobs around the great establishment; and in emergency to manufacture quantities of lance heads and arbalist [crossbow] bolts, as well as perhaps to provide the metal work for siege engines. . . . [He] is accordingly one of the most important and best rewarded of all the servitors.[88]

For such exacting tasks as fashioning chain mail hauberks, the baron might employ a special armorer.

To fulfill the multitude of other daily tasks around the castle, there were dozens of menials, or unskilled workers, such as watchmen and porters, carters and grooms, gardeners and huntsmen. Some menials were permanent employees; others were brought in on a temporary basis to tackle large jobs such as a full-scale cleaning of the castle.

Child servants occupied the lowest rungs of the household hierarchy, taking orders from everyone above them. Despite this, there was no shortage of applicants for these jobs, since they could easily lead to more desirable positions. If a boy from a peasant family worked diligently enough, he might manage to work his way up to the status of a gentleman or even achieve knighthood. But even if he did not advance that far, in most cases he was probably better off working inside the castle than he would have been on the outside.

The Benefits of Being Inside

Wages, even for important members of a lord's household, could not be considered generous. While an unskilled laborer hired temporarily might earn two pence a day and a skilled carpenter or mason twice that much, household servants were more likely to receive only a penny a day—about a pound and a half per year. And, like their masters, they were expected to give a percentage of that away again in the form of offerings to the church or alms for the poor.

Of course, there were other benefits to being a member of a lord's household. A castle servant always had a place to sleep, even if it was only on a palliasse, or straw mat, spread out on the floor or on the straw in the stable. In addition, it was customary for all members of the household, even important officials, to

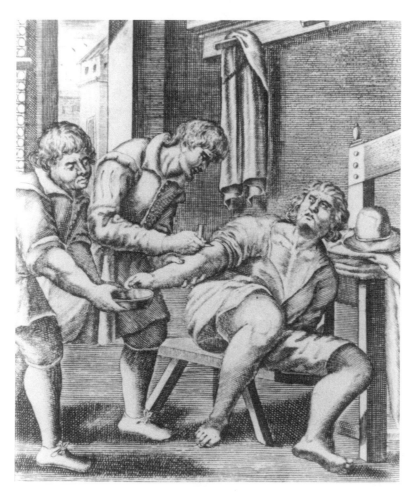

In addition to cutting hair, castle barbers also practiced medicine and were able to let blood, a practice that was believed to improve one's health.

A lord pays a visit to his highly esteemed armorers, who are busily plying their trade in preparation for war.

receive clothing and perhaps shoes as part of their wages. This bonus was ordinarily handed out at Christmastime.

Castle employees always had plenty to eat, too, except on those rare occasions when the castle was under a prolonged siege. They enjoyed more or less the same fare as their master, with a couple of exceptions. The bread at the lower table was not the finest white *wastel*, but more likely the heavy whole wheat stuff—which, of course, was far healthier, though they were probably not aware of the fact.

Instead of wine—the nobles' overwhelming favorite—common men had to make do with ale, a malt beverage similar to beer but darker and stronger tasting. They must not have minded much, for ale was consumed in vast quantities, especially in England. In some households the standard daily allowance of ale for each man was a gallon or even two gallons a day! Judging from the lyrics of one medieval song, in some quarters ale was considered more essential even than bread:

> Bring us in no brown bread, for that is made of bran,
>
> Nor bring us in no white bread, for therein is no game.

But bring us in good ale, and bring us in good ale;

For our blessed Lady's sake, bring us in good ale![89]

Staying in Service

Since most of the basic necessities of life were provided for them, thrifty servants could put aside most of what they earned. In fact, a frugal servant could build up a small fortune over many years of service, especially if his master supplemented his salary with rewards, tips, and holiday bonuses. Some lords even granted pensions to their most loyal longtime servants.

Once a servant obtained a comfortable position in a household, he was likely to hold onto it. Examples of men who put in twenty years in the service of one lord are not unusual. Of course, some lords were more pleasant to work for than others. Several of the wealthiest lords had reputations as harsh masters who were abusive and suspicious of their servants. Disagreements among the household members themselves sometimes made for unpleasant working conditions, too.

Ordinarily the duties themselves were not all that demanding, thanks to the large number of hands available to perform them. Often the workday was divided into three shifts—morning, afternoon, and evening—so that few servants had to put in a full day. Even those servants in positions of responsibility seldom worked more than a total of four or five hours each day.

In any case, no matter how much servants might toil or how trying their lives might become, members of a castle household could count themselves lucky. As Anthony Kemp observes,

Those living there . . . even the humblest, were often better off than those outside. They were never likely to go short of food and clothing, and had the advantage of belonging to a group with a certain *esprit de corps* [feeling of unity]. . . . Looking down from the lofty walls, they could afford to disdain the wretched civilians below.[90]

"Alas What Will Become of Me?"

Not all "civilians" were equally wretched, of course. As with the nobles and their servants,

Ale and Wassail

Ale, the commoner's drink, was made from the same grains as the commoner's bread. Because it could be brewed in great quantities inexpensively, even a poor peasant could afford to drink enough of it to make him mellow or even a bit silly. Urban Tigner Holmes Jr. writes about the drink in *Daily Living in the Twelfth Century,*

"Englishmen, when they got together, practiced the silly custom of 'Wassail! Drink-Hail!' The first drinker would pick up a 'mazer,' or bowl of bird's eye maple . . . salute his companion with a kiss, and cry 'Wassail!' The other bestowed a kiss in turn and cried the other word. They both drank. A great deal of humor was displayed in this, and it is easy to guess that a drinker's legs would not stand up under much of it. The people on the Continent observed this practice with awe and amusement, and were disposed to consider the English to be drunkards because of it."

the local peasants, or villeins, experienced various degrees of comfort and wealth—or lack of them.

The lowest of the low, called the *ribauz*, were vagrants who made their living, such as it was, either by begging or by following in the wake of an army and claiming whatever plunder the knights left behind. "They hung around outside the door of the banquet hall when a large feast was held," writes Urban Tigner Holmes Jr. "Frequently in twelfth-century romances a beautiful damsel is threatened with the awful fate of being turned over to the *ribauz*."[91]

A bit farther up the social scale were the serfs and, above them, the freemen. Though men of both classes had a roof over their heads and a bit of land to farm, they paid heavy dues to the local lord, either in the form of labor or in the form of rents and taxes.

A complex feudal system kept serfs fettered to the land and indebted to their lord. In return for land to farm, these servile peasants were required to pay their lord in the form of taxes, rent, or labor.

Some peasants were relatively prosperous, but the majority lived hand to mouth—and often not for very long. Life expectancy among the lower classes was short due to overwork, overexposure to the elements, and illness. In the French tale *Merlin Merlot*, a peasant speaks for much of his class when he cries, "Alas what will become of me who has never had a single day's rest? I do not think I shall ever know repose or ease. . . . Hard is the hour when the villein is born. When he is born, suffering is born with him."[92]

The nobility held the peasants in contempt, regarding them as brutish, sullen, and stupid, or, alternatively, as shrewd, suspicious, and tricky. In turn, the peasants resented the nobles for taking so much of the little they had and making such poor use of it. Jean de Venette, a medieval writer, observed that the common people "groaned to see dissipated in games and ornaments the sums they had so painfully furnished for the needs of war."[93]

Give and Take

The relationship between civilian and castle was, however, not just a matter of one side giving and the other taking. In fact, the presence of a noble household in a rural area had decided benefits. Not only did it create jobs for many of the locals, it also provided an economic stimulus to the whole region by giving farmers a ready market for their excess crops.

The castle also, of course, provided a measure of security. In peacetime the common people—except for those who worked in the household—were ordinarily excluded from the castle. Even if they had a petition for the lord, or a complaint, it often had to be heard at a court held outside the castle gates.

But in wartime common folk from the surrounding area expected to be able to take refuge within the castle walls. They were not always made welcome, though. On one occasion peasants who took shelter in Bamburgh Castle in England complained that an official "charged them 12d [pence] for each plot of ground within the castle where they could store their personal belongings." In addition, "the gate-keepers demanded fees for their access and exit."[94]

Defending a Way of Life

The commoners who sought sanctuary in the castle were also apparently expected to contribute by helping keep watch on the walls. The castle staff might be even more actively involved in its defense. An account of the life of the French knight Bertrand du Guesclin described an attack he made on a castle that was being defended by its servants. Du Guesclin and his men, disguised as woodcutters, were admitted through the gates. When the invaders' identities were discovered,

> Down rushed the English in hot wrath, full a hundred men in all—cooks and turnspits, boys and varlets, and good men at arms: they came about Bertrand like bees, and cast great flint-stones to smite him down. . . . An English squire raised his axe and smote one of Bertrand's comrades on the ear. . . . Bertrand seized the axe. . . . He drove the English into a sheep-pen; there was he shut in on every side with cooks and buttery-boys, pantlers and grooms and suchlike rabble; one wielded a pitchfork, another a pointed pole; many a shrewd stroke he had from spit and pestle. . . . Then . . . up rode a troop of horse[men]. . . . They slew outright all that they

Commoners were assured refuge within their lord's castle during wartime; however, they, along with the castle's appointed garrison, were expected to defend the fortress from attack.

found in the castle . . . and sent for wine to pass around among themselves.[95]

What motivated these men and boys, who were neither trained for battle nor equipped for it, to risk their lives? Loyalty played a large part, certainly. But there was surely a selfish consideration at work, too: The servants knew that, in order for their life of relative ease and comfort to continue, the castle had to remain in the hands of its lord. They were simply doing their best to ensure that it did.

Life in Wartime

When stone castles began to dominate the landscape of continental Europe and England in the twelfth century, they changed the nature of warfare. Large forces no longer clashed in full-scale battles. Instead, as historian N. J. G. Pounds explains,

> The appearance of a hostile army was followed by retreat into the castle and re-emergence when the danger had passed. There were skirmishes and ambushes, but battles were rare. The forces engaged were small, and warfare consisted largely in destroying whatever resources might be useful to the other side; in protecting oneself in one's own castle, and in attacking the enemy in his.[96]

Once the object of making war had been to defeat an opposing lord's army—which inevitably meant losing many of one's own men in the process. Now the object was to weaken an adversary's control and strengthen one's own by capturing the enemy's stronghold, his base of operations. Even Richard I of England, who was considered a great warrior, fought no more than two or three actual battles in his career, but he was involved in innumerable sieges. He died, in fact, from an injury he received while trying to capture a castle.

By the thirteenth century, castle walls had become so high and massive, and the methods of defending them so sophisticated, that the advantage lay overwhelmingly with the garrison inside rather than with the attackers. Presuming that they had enough advance warning, the occupants of the castle hurriedly brought in enough provisions and water to endure a long siege, stockpiled weapons, and cleared the surrounding land of anything that might shelter or supply the enemy. As soon as an approaching army was sighted, the drawbridge was drawn up and the gates were fastened.

Attackers' Alternatives

Bringing down a well-prepared stronghold, especially one surrounded by a moat or by concentric fortifications, or both, was often an impossible task. At best it was an extremely drawn out and expensive one. Stirling Castle in Scotland held out against its besiegers for most of the year 1299. Expenses incurred by the forces who laid siege to England's Bedford Castle in 1224 came to over thirteen hundred pounds.

Attackers basically had five options: They could climb the wall; they could breach, or break, the walls, either by pounding them with artillery or by undermining them; they could set fire to the buildings in the bailey; they could starve out the garrison; or they could resort to more devious methods such as trickery or treachery.

Escalade—using wooden or rope ladders to scale the walls—was the simplest tactic and, if it succeeded, the quickest. But it was also the riskiest. The attackers were liable to lose a lot of men in the attempt. As Anthony Kemp explains,

The scaling ladder thrown up against the wall could easily be thrown down, and heads and fingers appearing on the parapet could quickly be lopped off. In addition, the intrepid climbers on the way up would have been subject to all the frightful things that could be thrown down on them—boiling liquids, quicklime, iron bars, rocks and red-hot sand.[97]

The French poet who recorded the exploits of Bertrand du Guesclin gave an account of an escalade attempt on the castle of Melun that was more farcical than fatal. Bertrand took up a ladder, "set it to up to the wall and seized a shield to cover his head." The defenders then

discharged a mighty herring-barrel full of stones plump upon Bertrand as he mounted his ladder. So boisterous was the blow that the ladder brake, and Bertrand

A Counterweight Drawbridge

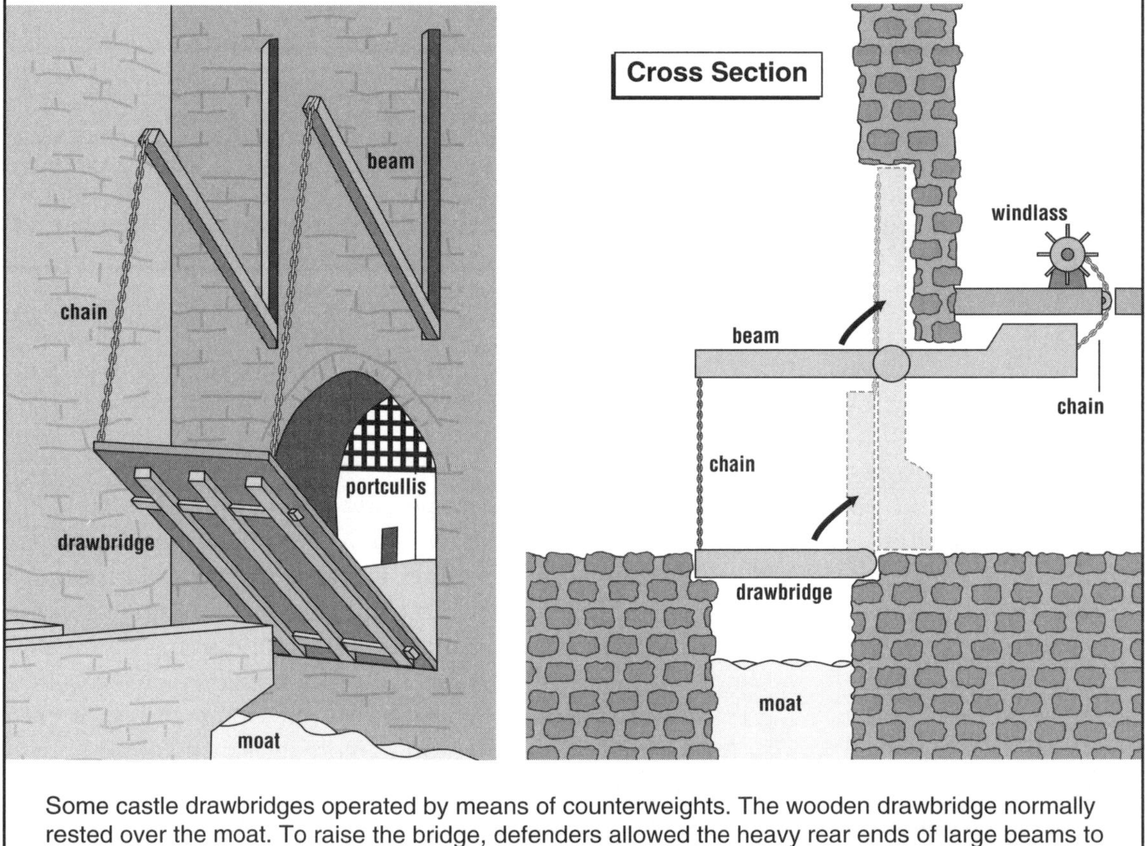

Cross Section

beam

chain

windlass

beam

chain

chain

portcullis

drawbridge

drawbridge

moat

moat

Some castle drawbridges operated by means of counterweights. The wooden drawbridge normally rested over the moat. To raise the bridge, defenders allowed the heavy rear ends of large beams to fall. As the lighter front ends rose, they raised the bridge by means of chains connecting the two.

While archers launch arrows, medieval knights battle their way onto an enemy castle's ramparts with the help of a belfry.

fell headlong . . . into the moat. . . . Thus he tarried awhile with his two feet in the air. . . . Then came a squire and . . . dragged him forth from the water. Forth came Bertrand's head all covered with mud; so stunned was he that he knew not where he was. . . . Forth from thence they bore him by main force, and laid him for his comfort within a warm dung-heap, until he came to himself again.[98]

Engines of War

A more sophisticated and time-consuming method of escalade was to build a *beffroi*, or belfry—a wooden tower the same height as the castle walls. The *Lanercost Chronicle*, compiled by medieval friars, describes how, at the siege of Carlisle, England, the attacking Scots

set up a great Belfry, like a tower, which far overtopped the town walls; whereupon the city carpenters . . . built another tower of wood that overtopped that belfry. But the Scottish engine never came against the wall; for when men dragged it on its wheels over the wet and miry ground, there it stuck fast with its own weight.[99]

If an escalade was not successful, the attackers settled in for a long siege. Often they threw up fortifications of their own, usually earthworks topped with a wooden palisade, to protect their encampment.

Then the attackers most likely set about building a huge machine called a siege engine, or perhaps several of them, that would enable them to fire missiles at or over the enemy's walls. Frequently a master engineer was brought in to design these engines and to oversee their construction and use. Expert engineer Brother Robert of Ulm was paid the considerable sum of nine pence per day for his services at the siege of Caerlaverock, Scotland, in 1300. However, if there was not enough lumber on the site, a prebuilt engine might be brought in.

Mighty Machines

Though siege engines came in many styles and sizes and were known by a variety of names, the collective term for them was *petraria* or *perriers*, meaning "stone throwers." Most of these engines worked on the same basic principle as a fork in a food fight: A throwing arm was loaded with a missile of some sort and was then drawn back and let go, propelling the object at the enemy.

Some engines were capable of flinging a three-hundred-pound stone for a distance of up to two hundred yards, but the projectile did not always go that far. A machine used by the Scots in 1174 malfunctioned and, instead of delivering the stone to the enemy, dropped it directly on a soldier who was manning the engine.

In machines like the mangonel, the throwing arm was powered by ropes that were twisted tightly by a windlass, or winch, and then released. This type of engine was not very accurate and was best used to lob objects over the castle walls and into the bailey.

The throwing arm of the trebuchet and similar engines was more like a seesaw with a heavy weight at one end—usually a box full of lead, iron, rocks, or sand. When the business end was drawn down by a winch and then released, the missile, which was lighter than the weight, went flying. "These machines," wrote a fourteenth-century witness, "cast their missiles with the utmost exactness, because the weight acts in a uniform manner. Their aim is so sure, that one may, so to say, hit a needle."[100]

Some of these incredibly large and complex siege engines were so impressive that their builders gave them distinctive names such as the Parson or the Forester or the *Malvoisin*—French for "bad neighbor." One of the most massive on record, the English-built Warwolf, was built for the siege of Stirling Castle in 1304. Its construction took three months and occupied at times as many as five master carpenters and forty-nine ordinary laborers.

Stones were not the only objects flung by attackers into the castle. Other possible ammunition included the rotted carcasses of livestock—which were probably meant to spread disease among the garrison—and the severed heads of prisoners—which were used mainly as a psychological tactic.

The most dreaded payload of all was a flammable substance known as "Greek fire," which had been in use since the seventh century. Its exact ingredients are lost to history, but it probably consisted at least in part of naptha (distilled petroleum), sulphur, and pitch, or resin. Whatever it hit, it stuck to, and it could not be extinguished with water. It was usually packed into earthenware pots that shattered on impact, spreading the flaming contents about like a medieval equivalent of napalm.

Cannon and Giant Crossbows

A slightly different sort of siege engine from the *perriers* was the ballista, or springald, which resembled a huge crossbow. It shot a bolt four times the size of an arrow. A ninth-century monk who observed a ballista in action claimed that the bolt impaled three soldiers at once, like chickens on a spit.

The early years of the fourteenth century saw the advent of a new species of artillery, one that launched missiles not by machinery but by the explosive force of gunpowder, which had been introduced to Europe in 1250. These precursors of the cannon were not very accurate and were, in fact, often more dangerous to their own crews than they were to the enemy. The first guns, which fired an arrowlike bolt rather than a ball, were made of iron bars welded together and bound with iron hoops. They had an unfortunate tendency to blow up in the faces of the men firing them. An early history of Scotland recorded that, at the siege of Roxburgh Castle, King

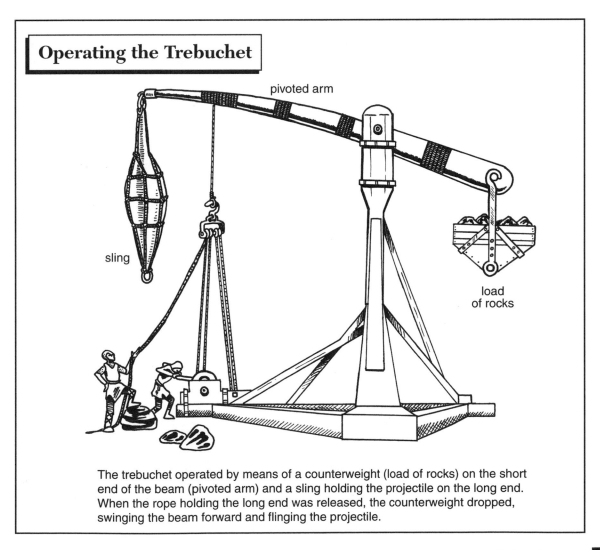

Operating the Trebuchet

pivoted arm

sling

load of rocks

The trebuchet operated by means of a counterweight (load of rocks) on the short end of the beam (pivoted arm) and a sling holding the projectile on the long end. When the rope holding the long end was released, the counterweight dropped, swinging the beam forward and flinging the projectile.

James II "did stand near the gunners when the artillery discharged: his thigh bone was dung in two with the piece of a misformed gun that brake in shooting, by which he was stricken to the ground and died hastily."[101]

Cannon would not develop sufficiently to pose much threat to massive stone walls until the late fourteenth century. In the meantime, besiegers relied mainly on machines or on human power.

"The Sow Has Farrowed!"

Occasionally soldiers might muscle a battering ram—usually a massive tree trunk tipped with iron and placed on wheels—up to the walls or the gate while under the cover of a movable protective shed called a "cat" or a "sow." "It is constructed," wrote William of Malmesbury in the eleventh century, "of slight timbers, the roof covered with boards and wicker-work and the sides protected with undressed hides."[102]

At the siege of Berwick, Scotland, in 1319, bales of burning wood and tar were dropped on a sow that was shielding English soldiers. When the invaders came scurrying out from under the flaming shelter, the Scottish defenders cried, "The sow has farrowed [given birth]!"[103]

Another sort of movable shelter called a *pavis*, which was used by the archers or crossbowmen of the attacking force, was basically just a large curved shield that could stand upright on the ground. A larger version with a prop that made it more stable was called a mantelet.

Miners, who were often called sappers, also went about their work under the cover of protective shelters. Though their methods required much time and patience, they were

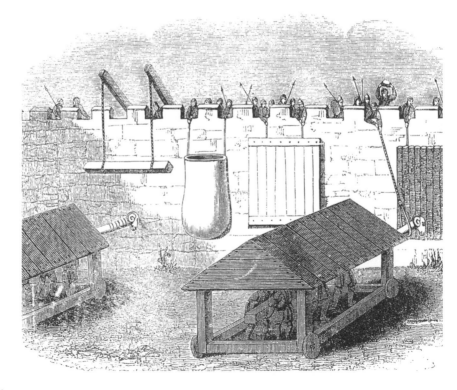

As enemy soldiers approach under a sow, a besieged castle garrison lowers sacks and wooden panels to absorb the impact of the battering rams.

The Castle of Hate

In the same way that some nobles staged tournaments that were more in the nature of a spectacle than a battle, others concocted elaborate mock sieges. G. G. Coulton's *Life in the Middle Ages* includes a passage from a thirteenth-century writer describing how a whimsical "Castle of Love" at an Italian court inspired hatred among its besiegers.

"A fantastic castle was built and garrisoned with dames and damsels and their waiting-women, who without help of man defended it with all possible prudence. . . . And the arms and engines wherewith men fought against it were apples and dates and muscat-nuts, tarts and pears and quinces, roses and lilies and violets. . . . Yet much evil may spring sometimes from good beginnings; for, while the Venetians strove in sport with the Paduans, contending who should first press into the castle gate, then discord arose. . . . A certain unwise Venetian . . . made an assault upon the Paduans with fierce and wrathful mein; which when the Paduans saw, some of them waxed wroth . . . which again provided the Venetians to sore wrath and indignation. So the Court or pastime was forthwith broken up. . . . In process of time the enmity between Paduans and Venetians waxed so sore that all commerce of trade was forbidden on either side . . . so that discord grew afresh, and wars, and deadly enmity."

usually more effective and less costly, both in terms of money and of lives, than a direct assault on the walls with ladders, siege engines, or battering rams.

Digging Dirt

The technique of undermining—digging dirt from beneath a wall until it collapsed—had been in use as far back as 510 B.C. As defensive walls grew thicker, though, they became more difficult to undermine, especially if they were surrounded by a moat full of water.

The usual procedure was to excavate under the weakest or most poorly defended section of a wall. Miners would first shore up the tunnel with timbers and then set the supporting timbers alight. When England's King John laid siege to the great tower at Rochester in 1215, he employed a more unorthodox method. Once his sappers had tunneled under a corner of the tower, the king sent an urgent message to one of his officers ordering him to provide "with all speed forty of the fattest pigs of the sort least good for eating."[104] When the pigs arrived on the scene, they were promptly killed; the carcasses were crammed between the supports in the tunnel and set on fire. After the fat on the corpses had burned for hours, the supports gave way and the tower wall above collapsed, leaving a gaping hole through which the king's men poured.

If the walls of a castle were particularly thick, the miners might tunnel under them, instead of trying to bring them down, and emerge in the bailey or even inside the tower. A long tunnel like this had its drawbacks, aside from the amount of time required to dig it. At the siege of a Welsh castle by English forces in 1287, Lord Stafford and a detachment of men were crawling through a tunnel when the earth above them caved in, suffocating the lord and his companions.

Countering the Attack

Naturally, while the attackers were engaged in trying to batter down the castle walls or undermine them, the defenders were not sitting around idly waiting. They were countering the attack with tactics and weapons of their own.

If the enemy was in the process of digging a tunnel, the garrison was ordinarily aware of it. They might even set up a row of crude motion sensors in the form of bowls full of water, which rippled in response to vibrations from below, or copper basins containing lead balls that rattled.

When the defenders had determined roughly where the mining was taking place, they might set sappers of their own to work digging a countermine that would, if they were skilled enough or fortunate enough, intercept the enemy's tunnel.

If the attackers employed a battering ram against the wall or the gate, the defenders lowered padded sacks on ropes to absorb the blows of the ram. If the besieging forces tried to undermine or scale the walls or fill in a section of the moat with brush and timbers to create a makeshift bridge, the soldiers stationed atop the walls rained missiles down upon them.

One of the writers of the *Lanercost Chronicle* recorded that, at the siege of Carlisle, the defenders "cast upon them from the wall javelins and arrows and stones . . . in such multitude and number that they [the attackers] enquired one of the other 'Do stones increase and multiply, then, within these walls?'"[105]

Hoardings and Murder Holes

At the siege of Tourfière, France, the women who had taken refuge in the castle stood on the battlements alongside the men, casting stones as well as burning pitch and boiling water on the troops below.

To make it easier for the garrison to dump these deadly materials on the heads of the opposing army, the owners of many early castles built a wooden catwalk, called a hoarding or brattice, that projected from the top of the walls like a continuous balcony. The hoarding was roofed over for protection, and the floor had gaps in it through which projectiles and liquids could be dropped.

Wooden hoardings were, of course, vulnerable to fire and could be smashed by a well-aimed shot from a siege engine. Later castles incorporated galleries made of stone, called machicolations, into their designs.

The area of the wall above the main gate was commonly provided with "murder holes" that allowed soldiers to pour scalding water or molten lead on the enemy or, if the gates were set afire, to douse the flames with water.

The garrison also had weapons that could deliver death to the enemy at a distance. They might build a mangonel, a trebuchet, or a ballista of their own, though the machines would have had to be on a smaller scale if they were to be placed atop the walls. The defenders' archers and crossbowmen, however, were their deadliest resources.

The Deadly Crossbow

The crossbow, or arbalest, was especially effective. Though its rate of fire was slower than that of the ordinary longbow, it was remarkably accurate up to a distance of four hundred yards or so. In addition, it was so powerful that its wooden bolts, called quarrels, could pierce armor.

So deadly was the crossbow, in fact, that in 1139 the church condemned its use—without

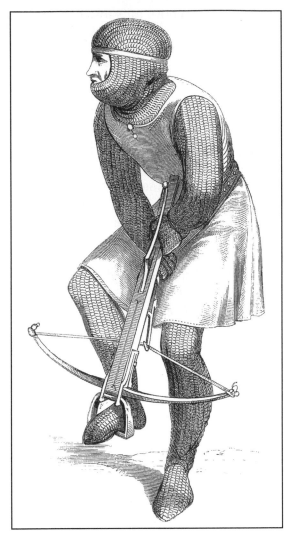

A crossbowman places his right foot in a stirrup while securing the bowstring. Crossbowmen were hired mercenaries.

bowman to hold down the weapon while the bowstring was hauled into place. Another kind was *à tour,* in which the bowstring was stretched with the aid of a cord, hooked to the man's belt, and a pulley. The bow itself was of composite construction, using horn and wood.[106]

A later version of the weapon had a bow made of steel. Crossbowmen were neither knights nor ordinary foot soldiers but were specialized mercenaries, or hired fighting men, who sold their expertise to the highest bidder. They did not come cheap. A crossbowman might earn from four to six pence per day, far more than a lowly infantryman.

Archers and crossbowmen who were stationed in the tower of a castle fired their weapons through narrow loopholes, or arrow slits, usually cross-shaped ones that allowed the bowman a range of motion from side to side as well as up and down.

A bowman whose post was on the battlements concealed himself behind the parapet—a stone extension six to nine feet high that shielded the walkway that ran along the top of the walls. The parapet might be provided with arrow slits, or the bowman might fire through the embrasures, regularly spaced openings in the parapet that were two or three feet wide and were sometimes protected by hinged wooden shutters.

Sallies and Slaughter

Occasionally the lord of a castle under siege might grow impatient with always being on the defensive and lead a band of knights on a sally, riding out through the postern gate at the rear of the castle and taking the enemy by surprise from behind. Some castles were equipped with an underground passage leading to a

much effect. It was a favorite weapon of Richard I, who was, ironically, slain by a bolt from a crossbow. Michael Prestwich explains that

> crossbows were not all of the same design; some were described as with one foot, and others with two. This referred to the stirrup, or stirrups, used by the cross-

The peasants who farmed the land in the vicinity of a castle were likely to suffer far more from a war than the castle's defenders did. As Morris Bishop notes in his book *The Middle Ages*, the attacking army's purpose "was not to defeat the enemy but rather to harm him by burning his villages, massacring his peasants, destroying his source of income, while he raged impotently but securely in his castle. 'When two nobles quarrel,' wrote a contemporary, "the poor man's thatch goes up in flames.'" Bishop goes on to quote an epic poem of the period that describes how an attacking army employed the strategy of *chevauchée*, or ravaging the countryside.

"[They] set the villages on fire, and the foragers visit and sack them. The distracted inhabitants are burnt or led apart with their hands tied to be held for ransom. Everywhere alarm bells ring, fear spreads from side to side and becomes general. . . . Here hands are laid on money; there cattle, donkeys, and flocks are seized. The smoke spreads, the flames rise, the peasants and the shepherds in consternation flee in all directions."

secret "sally port" that, in an extreme situation, might also be used as an escape route.

Rather than risk their men's lives in hand-to-hand fighting, most castle owners preferred to sit tight and trust that the massive stone walls of their stronghold would stand up against anything the enemy threw at them. The enemy, however, had other, more devious tactics. When a castle fell, it was usually not as a result of a direct offensive but rather through surrender or treachery.

One strong motive for surrender was impending starvation. No matter how huge the lord's stockpile of provisions, it could not last indefinitely. The men outside the walls did not have an unlimited supply of food, either. It did not take them long to deplete the surrounding countryside of the few crops and animals that remained. Medieval armies had no organized system for furnishing food and supplies; they relied mainly on what they could buy or steal in the immediate area.

Although the attackers, if they were really determined, could cart in supplies from elsewhere, the defenders had no such option. If they ran short of supplies, the most they could hope for was that an ally might come to their aid and rout the besieging forces. If that did not happen, the garrison had no choice but to surrender.

For all but the most prideful lord, surrender was preferable to starving to death or having the castle taken by force—in which case the defenders might be hanged or killed outright. "Whenever a castle was yielded," writes N. J. G. Pounds, "the garrison was usually allowed to march away. Only when it was taken by assault do we find evidence of a wholesale slaughter."[107]

One example of "wholesale slaughter" occurred when Edward, prince of Wales, took the castle at Limoges, France, in 1370. He was so angry over the resistance shown him that he had three hundred men, women, and children beheaded. "It was a great pity," writes Jean Froissart, "to see them kneeling before the prince, begging for mercy; but he took no heed of them."[108]

Giving Up the Game

Still, having to surrender could be humiliating. After the Scots who held Stirling Castle in 1304 gave themselves up, they were forced to march out of the stronghold barefoot and with ashes heaped on their heads.

While the surrender of Stirling was an unconditional one, the defenders usually negotiated in advance with the attackers and agreed upon terms. Often these negotiations became, according to Pounds, "a kind of poker game governed by strict rules. In the siege of Dolforwyn 'the garrison gave eight hostages . . . as a guarantee that they will surrender the castle on the Thursday after the close of Easter unless they are relieved . . . and if they are relieved, the hostages are to be returned to them.'"[109]

The siege of Stirling mentioned above resembled a game even more. The English army, under the command of Edward I, had a special viewing gallery constructed so that the ladies of the court could watch the proceedings like spectators at a sporting match. Ed-ward also had the giant siege engine Warwolf built for the occasion. When the Scots offered to surrender, the king refused to accept because he had not yet had an opportunity to try out his expensive machine. Only after the Warwolf had succeeded in caving in a large section of the castle wall was the garrison permitted to yield.

Though starving an enemy into submission was, in terms of lives lost, at least, better than an all-out attack, there was an even quicker and more bloodless way of bringing down a castle. Rather than overpowering his enemy, or outwaiting him, the resourceful commander looked for a way to outwit him.

Trickery and Treachery

For a long time after its construction, Château Gaillard in France, with its thick concentric

Scotland's Stirling Castle, as it appeared prior to its devastating siege. The castle's inhabitants surrendered to the English army in 1304.

walls, was considered impregnable. Between 1203 and 1204 the English captured and defended it successfully against the French for six months. Though the attackers breached the outer bailey wall, the middle and inner baileys might have held out indefinitely if it had not been for a bit of subterfuge. A French soldier searched the river bank below the castle until he came upon the outlet drain from the latrines. He proceeded to crawl up the drainpipe—gagging all the way, no doubt—and, once inside, lowered the drawbridge for his fellow soldiers.

England's Devizes Castle was captured by Robert Fitz Hubert, a Flemish mercenary who used scaling ladders made of leather for silence. He and his men entered the castle without attracting any notice and captured the sleeping garrison.

In the fourteenth century, Scotland's Robert Bruce proved himself a master in the art of surprise attack. Bruce and his men captured the castle at Perth by wading through the icy waters of the moat and then climbing the walls on scaling ladders.

Other castles fell as a result of trickery or treachery. A few armed men might be hidden in a hay cart and smuggled into a castle in advance so that they would be in a position to open the gate for the main army when it arrived.

Forgery was another possibility. At the siege of the Krak des Chevaliers in the Holy Land, the besiegers showed the castellan, the officer in charge of the castle, a letter that purported to be from his lord commanding him to surrender. The castellan obeyed, only to discover that the letter was a fake. Such an official might also be induced to surrender his lord's castle by the offer of a bribe.

Though there obviously was no such thing as a truly impregnable stronghold, by the end of the thirteenth century the art of castle building had outstripped the art of laying siege to them. Even the introduction of cannon in the late fourteenth century did not pose a substantial threat, at least not at first. During the siege of the castle at Ypres, Belgium, in 1383, two cannon fired a total of more than four hundred shots without injuring a single one of the castle's defenders.

It would take a more subtle and sweeping influence to bring the heyday of the castle to an end. It would take, in fact, nothing less than the long, slow erosion and eventual collapse of the feudal system itself.

The Decline of the Castle

Ironically the ability of castles to withstand a prolonged siege was one of the factors that led ultimately to their downfall. Under the feudal system, a knight was obliged to fight for his lord only forty days at a stretch, but a well-built and well-provisioned castle might hold out for six months or a year. Obviously, a lord who was in the midst of a siege could not depend on soldiers who, when their tour of duty was up, could just ride off.

So, over time, knights who were bound to a lord by nothing but loyalty began to play a smaller and smaller role in warfare. At the same time, the role played by mercenaries grew ever larger. Increasingly, as Jay Williams explains,

> the real fate of the battle rested on the pikemen, the archers, and finally the gunners. Regular pay and plenty of it was more important than duty or honor, and well-paid soldiers could be kept in the field as long as money could be found for them. . . . Knights began hiring themselves out as mercenaries, wandering from the pay of one master to that of another.[110]

Mercenaries, particularly those employed as archers and gunners, began to replace loyalty-bound knights in both the defense and siege of castles.

For a mounted soldier, the pay could be substantial—from two shillings a day in the thirteenth century to as much as fifteen shillings a day a century later. A knight-banneret, who had the authority to hire mercenaries of his own, might receive twice that much.

Many lords employed an indenture system, under which knights were bound to serve them for a specific period of time in return for a specified sum, typically fifty to one hundred pounds for a year's service.

"The Drudges of War"

The pay received by ordinary foot soldiers, of course, was only a fraction of a knight's wages. Often they made up for it by plundering the countryside. As historian Georges Duby writes,

> Such mercenaries were the drudges of war. . . . The vast majority came from wild and impoverished regions. . . . They were a permanent grouping, and continued to roam, pillaging and living off the land, when they were not receiving wages . . . and spread fear wherever they went. . . . Yet . . . a lord rich enough to employ these companies found it difficult to defend his lands without them.[111]

As lords relied more and more on mercenaries, the nature of feudalism changed. Instead of a family-like structure held together by mutual loyalties and obligations, it became an economic system based on the payment of wages.

Just as the advent of the castle had changed the nature of warfare in the twelfth century, the new importance of mercenaries began to change it again. Due to the increasing cost of maintaining a castle and an army, power became concentrated in the hands of just a few of the wealthiest nobles instead of being spread among a multitude of lesser ones.

With a greater number of men at their command who were available on a permanent year-round basis, these great lords could wage military campaigns that lasted months and included full-scale battles. The ability to defend a castle became less important than the ability to command an army in the field.

The Power of the State

The money-based economy had even more far-reaching effects. According to Duby,

> Money circulation affected the whole of society and made it much more flexible; but its importance was also profoundly destabilizing. . . . The individual enjoyed a new-found freedom. He held his own purse-strings. A son's expectations no longer depended solely on his father . . . or a knight's upon the lord in whose household he was brought up. He could take his chance outside the established group. . . . He needed to be able to refer to laws which operated outside the confines of household, village and castle. . . . What he required, in other words, was the power of the State.[112]

In the latter part of the Middle Ages, "the power of the State," represented by royalty, began to reassert itself. The kings of England and France took back much of the authority that had been usurped by various local barons. When the king's courts and its officials began to play a larger role in administering justice, the castle as a seat of local authority lost its importance.

A Residence That Could Be Defended

As a central authority regained control, the number of private quarrels between rival barons declined. And as the threat of war relaxed, the owners and builders of castles became less concerned with defense and more with livability. Instead of full-fledged fortresses, more and more barons began constructing something known as the "fortified manor house."

Though it had thick walls of brick or stone and often had towers complete with parapets and arrow slits or gun ports, the fortified manor house was a self-contained structure without a bailey or a surrounding wall. It was, in other words, a residence that could be defended rather than a stronghold that could be lived in.

In addition, many existing castles were converted into more comfortable residences. Others were abandoned and allowed to decay or were pulled down so the materials could be used for constructing new buildings.

The castles of France, which had lost much of their strategic importance thanks to a long period of peace in the early fourteenth century, got a new lease on life during the Hundred Years' War with England (1337–1453). Afterward, however, they continued their decline.

As the prominence of castles diminished, barons began constructing fortified manor houses, although few featured surrounding walls like this residence.

Flat Earth

Long before the English Civil War, rulers were in the habit of tearing down castles whose owners dared to defy their authority. After Henry III successfully stormed the motte and bailey at Bedford in 1224, he ordered it completely destroyed. In *The Medieval Castle in England and Wales,* N. J. G. Pounds details Henry's instructions.

"The bailey walls were to be flattened and the ditches filled and everything reduced to *plana terra* [flat earth]. The walls of the court upon the motte were to be lowered and their crenellations destroyed, and what remained was returned to William de Beauchamp, with leave to build there a *mansionem* [manor house] if he so wished. . . . Stone from the castle was given to rebuild St Paul's church in compensation for that removed to make missiles. Today the base only of the motte stands in a public park, its summit 49 m [meters] in diameter and rising 7½ m above the level ground.

Some of the castles in England, too, temporarily resumed their military function when the English Civil War broke out in 1642. But in the wake of the war, the English Parliament decided that the castles that had posed the greatest threats should be dismantled so that they could never be used for military purposes again. This process of destroying castles was known as "slighting."

Those castles that survived have met a variety of fates. Some have been converted into public buildings such as prisons and power stations. Others have fallen into states of ruin. Still others have been carefully restored by either private owners or their country's government and are open to visitors on a regular basis.

Several of the castles mentioned in this book are still wholly or mostly intact: the Tower of London, Stirling Castle in Scotland, and the Krak des Chevaliers in Syria. Little remains of others, such as France's Château Gaillard. But even walking through the ruins of a medieval castle can give a strong sense of what the landscape and the way of life were like when castles dominated them.

Notes

Introduction: The Feudal Family

1. Morris Bishop, *The Middle Ages.* Boston: Houghton Mifflin, 1968, p. 13.
2. Barbara W. Tuchman, *A Distant Mirror: The Calamitous 14th Century.* New York: Ballantine, 1978, p. 5.
3. Marc Bloch, *Feudal Society.* Chicago: University of Chicago Press, 1961, p. 148.
4. Clara and Richard Winston, *The Horizon Book of Daily Life in the Middle Ages.* New York: American Heritage, 1975, p. 47.
5. Bishop, *The Middle Ages,* pp. 109–10.
6. Georges Duby, *France in the Middle Ages, 987–1460: From Hugh Capet to Joan of Arc.* Oxford: Blackwell, 1991, p. 67.
7. Bishop, *The Middle Ages,* p. 110.

Chapter 1: The Rise of the Castle

8. Joan Evans, *Life in Medieval France.* London: Phaidon, 1969, p. 23.
9. Quoted in Evans, *Life in Medieval France,* p. 23.
10. Quoted in G. G. Coulton, ed., *Life in the Middle Ages.* New York: Macmillan, 1935, p. 37.
11. N. J. G. Pounds, *The Medieval Castle in England and Wales: A Social and Political History.* Cambridge: Cambridge University Press, 1990, p. 51.
12. Anthony Kemp, *Castles in Colour.* Poole, England: Blandford, 1977, pp. 94–96.
13. Quoted in Pounds, *The Medieval Castle in England and Wales,* p. 7.
14. Quoted in Pounds, *The Medieval Castle in England and Wales,* p. 9.

15. Quoted in Georges Duby, ed., *A History of Private Life: Revelations of the Medieval World.* Cambridge, MA: Belknap, 1988, p. 411.
16. Plantagenet Somerset Fry, *The David & Charles Book of Castles.* North Pomfret, VT: David & Charles, 1980, p. 109.
17. Tuchman, *A Distant Mirror,* p. 5.
18. Quoted in Bloch, *Feudal Society,* pp. 300–301.

Chapter 2: A Town Within Walls

19. William Stearns Davis, *Life on a Mediaeval Barony: A Picture of a Typical Feudal Community in the Thirteenth Century.* New York: Harper & Brothers, 1923, p. 46.
20. Margaret Wade Labarge, *A Baronial Household of the Thirteenth Century.* London: Eyre & Spottiswoode, 1965, p. 20.
21. Quoted in Pounds, *The Medieval Castle in England and Wales,* p. 194.
22. Quoted in Coulton, *Life in the Middle Ages,* p. 99.
23. Bloch, *Feudal Society,* p. 302.
24. Labarge, *A Baronial Household of the Thirteenth Century,* pp. 22–23.
25. Urban Tigner Holmes Jr., *Daily Living in the Twelfth Century: Based on the Observations of Alexander Neckam in London and Paris.* Madison: University of Wisconsin Press, 1952, p. 39.
26. Labarge, *A Baronial Household of the Thirteenth Century,* pp. 26–27.
27. Davis, *Life on a Mediaeval Barony,* p. 32.
28. Pounds, *The Medieval Castle in England and Wales,* p. 243.

29. Quoted in Labarge, *A Baronial Household of the Thirteenth Century*, p. 18.

30. Quoted in Evans, *Life in Medieval France*, p. 16.

Chapter 3: Lifestyles of the Rich and Noble

31. Tuchman, *A Distant Mirror*, p. 17.

32. Quoted in Davis, *Life on a Mediaeval Barony*, p. 42.

33. Evans, *Life in Medieval France*, p. 25.

34. Kate Mertes, *The English Noble Household, 1250–1600: Good Governance and Politic Rule*. Oxford: Basil Blackwell, 1988, p. 157.

35. Mertes, *The English Noble Household*, pp. 178–79.

36. Quoted in Holmes, *Daily Living in the Twelfth Century*, p. 251.

37. Quoted in Tuchman, *A Distant Mirror*, p. 17.

38. Quoted in Labarge, *A Baronial Household of the Thirteenth Century*, p. 105.

39. Quoted in Labarge, *A Baronial Household of the Thirteenth Century*, p. 111.

40. Quoted in Bloch, *Feudal Society*, p. 302.

41. Quoted in Labarge, *A Baronial Household of the Thirteenth Century*, p. 79.

42. Quoted in Coulton, *Life in the Middle Ages*, pp. 66–67.

43. Tuchman, *A Distant Mirror*, p. 234.

44. Quoted in Davis, *Life on a Mediaeval Barony*, p. 53.

45. Quoted in Davis, *Life on a Mediaeval Barony*, p. 55.

46. Holmes, *Daily Living in the Twelfth Century*, p. 43.

47. Quoted in Tuchman, *A Distant Mirror*, p. 16.

Chapter 4: The Lives of Women and Children

48. Tuchman, *A Distant Mirror*, p. 217.

49. Quoted in Labarge, *A Baronial Household of the Thirteenth Century*, p. 48.

50. Quoted in Labarge, *A Baronial Household of the Thirteenth Century*, p. 42.

51. Quoted in Labarge, *A Baronial Household of the Thirteenth Century*, p. 42.

52. Quoted in Coulton, *Life in the Middle Ages*, pp. 64–65.

53. Quoted in Jay Williams, *Life in the Middle Ages*. New York: Random House, 1966, p. 75.

54. Quoted in Coulton, *Life in the Middle Ages*, p. 84.

55. Quoted in Coulton, *Life in the Middle Ages*, p. 129.

56. Quoted in Coulton, *Life in the Middle Ages*, p. 138.

57. Labarge, *A Baronial Household of the Thirteenth Century*, p. 45.

58. Quoted in Coulton, *Life in the Middle Ages*, pp. 30–31.

59. Quoted in Tuchman, *A Distant Mirror*, pp. 50–51.

60. Quoted in Holmes, *Daily Living in the Twelfth Century*, p. 205.

61. Williams, *Life in the Middle Ages*, pp. 132–33.

62. Quoted in Evans, *Life in Medieval France*, p. 117.

63. Quoted in Frances and Joseph Gies, *Marriage and the Family in the Middle Ages*. New York: Harper & Row, 1987, p. 215.

64. Quoted in Gies, *Marriage and the Family in the Middle Ages*, pp. 212–13.

65. Quoted in Coulton, *Life in the Middle Ages*, p. 131.

66. Holmes, *Daily Living in the Twelfth Century*, p. 178.

Chapter 5: A Soldier's Life

67. Michael Prestwich, *Armies and Warfare in the Middle Ages: The English Experi-*

ence. New Haven, CT: Yale University Press, 1996, p. 26.

68. Williams, *Life in the Middle Ages*, p. 71.

69. Prestwich, *Armies and Warfare in the Middle Ages*, pp. 30–31.

70. Frances Gies, *The Knight in History*. New York: Harper & Row, 1984, p. 150.

71. Quoted in Prestwich, *Armies and Warfare in the Middle Ages*, p. 240.

72. Quoted in Bishop, *The Middle Ages*, p. 123.

73. Bloch, *Feudal Society*, p. 298.

74. Quoted in Coulton, *Life in the Middle Ages*, p. 254.

75. Quoted in Williams, *Life in the Middle Ages*, p. 84.

76. Williams, *Life in the Middle Ages*, pp. 84–86.

77. Quoted in Bishop, *The Middle Ages*, p. 77.

78. Quoted in Tuchman, *A Distant Mirror*, p. 63.

79. Quoted in Prestwich, *Armies and Warfare in the Middle Ages*, p. 220.

80. Quoted in Joan Evans, ed., *The Flowering of the Middle Ages*. New York: McGraw-Hill, 1966, p. 161.

81. Duby, *France in the Middle Ages*, p. 61.

Chapter 6: Life Among the Lowly

82. Mertes, *The English Noble Household*, p. 22.

83. Quoted in Labarge, *A Baronial Household of the Thirteenth Century*, pp. 59–60.

84. Mertes, *The English Noble Household*, pp. 63, 68.

85. Quoted in Labarge, *A Baronial Household of the Thirteenth Century*, p. 65.

86. Quoted in Tuchman, *A Distant Mirror*, p. 236.

87. Quoted in Tuchman, *A Distant Mirror*, p. 237.

88. Davis, *Life on a Mediaeval Barony*, pp. 26–27.

89. Quoted in Coulton, *Life in the Middle Ages*, p. 140.

90. Kemp, *Castles in Colour*, p. 177.

91. Holmes, *Daily Living in the Twelfth Century*, p. 37.

92. Quoted in Tuchman, *A Distant Mirror*, p. 174.

93. Quoted in Tuchman, *A Distant Mirror*, p. 176.

94. Quoted in Pounds, *The Medieval Castle in England and Wales*, p. 206.

95. Quoted in Coulton, *Life in the Middle Ages*, pp. 106–107.

Chapter 7: Life in Wartime

96. Pounds, *The Medieval Castle in England and Wales*, p. 44.

97. Kemp, *Castles in Colour*, p. 161.

98. Quoted in Coulton, *Life in the Middle Ages*, pp. 110–11.

99. Quoted in Coulton, *Life in the Middle Ages*, pp. 24–26.

100. Quoted in Edward L. Cutts, *Scenes and Characters of the Middle Ages*. Detroit: Singing Tree, 1968, p. 383.

101. Quoted in Fry, *The David & Charles Book of Castles*, p. 121.

102. Quoted in Cutts, *Scenes and Characters of the Middle Ages*, p. 386.

103. Quoted in Prestwich, *Armies and Warfare in the Middle Ages*, p. 291.

104. Quoted in Fry, *The David and Charles Book of Castles*, p. 71.

105. Quoted in Coulton, *Life in the Middle Ages*, p. 24.

106. Prestwich, *Armies and Warfare in the Middle Ages*, pp. 129–31.

107. Pounds, *The Medieval Castle in England and Wales*, p. 113.

108. Quoted in Bishop, *The Middle Ages*, p. 88.

109. Pounds, *The Medieval Castle in England and Wales*, p. 113.

Epilogue: The Decline of the Castle

110. Williams, *Life in the Middle Ages*, p. 109.

111. Duby, *France in the Middle Ages*, pp. 159–60.

112. Duby, *France in the Middle Ages*, pp. 161–63.

For Further Reading

Giovanni Caselli, *The Middle Ages*. New York: Peter Bedrick, 1988. Part of the *History of Everyday Things* series, this book is short on text, but full of detailed drawings of buildings, arms, armor, clothing, etc.

Denise Dersin, ed., *What Life Was Like in the Age of Chivalry: Medieval Europe AD 800–1500*. Alexandria, VA: Time-Life, 1997. A concise but comprehensive look at the church, the aristocracy, peasants, and town life. Heavily illustrated with medieval art and photos of period artifacts.

Carol Belanger Grafton, ed., *Medieval Life Illustrations*. New York: Dover, 1996. No text, just hundreds of black and white drawings and woodcuts that depict the everyday life of the three orders of medieval society.

Christopher Gravett, *Knight*. New York: Knopf, 1993.

———, *Castle*. New York: Knopf, 1994.

Andrew Langley, *Medieval Life*. New York: Knopf, 1996. These three titles, part of the popular *Eyewitness Books* series, use a combination of period art and photos of actual artifacts, plus reproductions of clothing and other items of the time, to give an unusually concrete picture of what the Middle Ages looked like.

Bryan Holme, *Medieval Pageant*. London: Thames and Hudson, 1987. Dozens of full-color period paintings and tapestries, accompanied by lengthy captions, that illustrate various aspects of medieval life.

Works Consulted

Morris Bishop, *The Middle Ages.* Boston: Houghton Mifflin, 1968. A very lucid and entertaining overview of the period from the Dark Ages to the Renaissance by a historian who was also a poet. Full of fascinating details and anecdotes, this book is illustrated with period pictures.

Marc Bloch, *Feudal Society.* Chicago: University of Chicago Press, 1961. Bloch, a French professor of medieval history, examines in depth the complex nature of feudal ties and the conditions that led to the development of the feudal system.

G. G. Coulton, ed., *Life in the Middle Ages.* New York: Macmillan, 1935. A treasure trove of excerpts from medieval manuscripts and documents, some rather obscure, that show how the world of the Middle Ages looked to the clerics and nobles who lived in it.

William Stearns Davis, *Life on a Mediaeval Barony: A Picture of a Typical Feudal Community in the Thirteenth Century.* New York: Harper & Brothers, 1923. An exhaustive examination of daily life on a fief, ranging from nobles to clergy to peasants. Davis tries to put the reader in the picture by using present tense and a casual writing style.

Georges Duby, *France in the Middle Ages, 987–1460: From Hugh Capet to Joan of Arc.* Oxford: Blackwell, 1991. Duby, one of France's most noted historians, covers the major events that shaped medieval France but also offers valuable insights into more everyday matters such as tournaments and finances.

Urban Tigner Holmes Jr., *Daily Living in the Twelfth Century: Based on the Observations of Alexander Neckam in London and Paris.* Madison: University of Wisconsin Press, 1952. Though Holmes mainly explores London and Paris, the information he provides sheds light on medieval lifestyles in general.

Margaret Wade Labarge, *A Baronial Household of the Thirteenth Century.* London: Eyre & Spottiswoode, 1965. An up-close and personal look at the day-to-day functioning of a medieval household, based on the domestic accounts of the countess of Leicester, sister of Henry III.

Kate Mertes, *The English Noble Household, 1250–1600: Good Governance and Politic Rule.* Oxford: Basil Blackwell, 1988. Like Labarge's book, this one draws on household accounts as well as other documents of the time to examine the living and working conditions of the lowest servants as well as their masters.

N. J. G. Pounds, *The Medieval Castle in England and Wales: A Social and Political History.* Cambridge: Cambridge University Press, 1990. A thoroughly researched and documented look at British castles, with the emphasis on their role as homes and administrative centers rather than as fortresses. The book includes maps, charts, and layouts of representative castles.

Michael Prestwich, *Armies and Warfare in the Middle Ages: The English Experience.* New Haven, CT: Yale University Press, 1996. An invaluable resource for specific information about siege warfare, arms, and armor. Prestwich gets beyond the chivalric image of the medieval knight to show how unromantic the life of a soldier really was and how important the ordinary foot soldier and engineer were in deciding the outcome of a battle.

Barbara W. Tuchman, *A Distant Mirror: The Calamitous 14th Century*. New York: Ballantine, 1978. This hefty book by a two-time Pulitzer Prize–winning historian was a best-seller when it was first published. Though it is well written and readable, it is also scholarly; Tuchman does not try to simplify history for popular consumption. She focuses mainly on the last half of the fourteenth century and on a single historical personage, a French knight named Enguerrand de Coucy VII.

Additional Works Consulted

Edward L. Cutts, *Scenes and Characters of the Middle Ages.* Detroit: Singing Tree, 1968.

Georges Duby, ed., *A History of Private Life: Revelations of the Medieval World.* Cambridge, MA: Belknap, 1988.

Joan Evans, ed., *The Flowering of the Middle Ages.* New York: McGraw-Hill, 1966.

Joan Evans, *Life in Medieval France.* London: Phaidon, 1969.

Plantagenet Somerset Fry, *The David & Charles Book of Castles.* North Pomfret, VT: David & Charles, 1980.

Frances Gies, *The Knight in History.* New York: Harper & Row, 1984.

Frances and Joseph Gies, *Marriage and the Family in the Middle Ages.* New York: Harper & Row, 1987.

Anthony Kemp, *Castles in Colour.* Poole, England: Blandford, 1977.

Marjorie Rowling, *Everyday Life of Medieval Travellers.* New York: Dorset, 1971.

Sidney Toy, *Castles: Their Construction and History.* New York: Dover, 1985.

Jay Williams, *Life in the Middle Ages.* New York: Random House, 1966.

Clara and Richard Winston, *The Horizon Book of Daily Life in the Middle Ages.* New York: American Heritage, 1975.

Index

abbots. *See* clergy
ale, 69, 72–73
Armies and Warfare in the Middle Ages (Prestwich), 64
armor, 59–60, 64, 84

baileys, 16, 17–18, 19, 20
  as small towns, 24–26
Bamburgh Castle (England), 75
barbarian tribes, 10
Baronial Household of the Thirteenth Century, A (Labarge), 60
barons, 12, 13, 19, 34
  as aggressors, 23
  income of, 20
  as judges, 37
  loyalty oaths of, 12
  see also knights; nobles
battering rams, 82, 84
beards, 35
Beauchamp, William de, 92
Bedford Castle (England), 77, 92
belfry, 79
Belgium, 15, 88
Berlichingen, Gotz von, 54–55
Berthelemy, Dominique, 21
Bishop, Morris, 11, 12, 14, 29
bishops. *See* clergy
blacksmiths, 25–26, 70
Bloch, Marc, 11, 26, 48, 61
Bonet, Honoré, 38
Born, Bertrand de, 44, 61
Bourbon, Etienne de, 48
bread, 40–41, 69, 72
Britain. *See* England
Brother Robert of Ulm, 80
Bruce, Robert, 88

candles, 26, 36

cannons, 81, 82, 88
castles, 15–33, 92
  attackers of, 77–88
    spectators of, 87
    undermined castle walls, 83–84
    used belfries, 79
    used escalades, 77–79
    used movable shelters, 82–83
    used siege engines, 80–81
    used starvation, 86, 87
    used trickery, 87–88
  behavioral standards in, 37–38, 40, 50
  chapels in, 30–31
  concentric fortifications of, 20, 77
  construction of, 16–17, 18, 19, 20–21, 30
  cost of, 20
  defenders of, 18, 77–78, 84–86, 91
    payments received by, 89–90
  design of, 15–16, 21, 26–28, 30, 84
  eating/dining in, 28, 34–35, 40–41
  fire hazards in, 18, 30
  food preparation in, 40, 69–70
  as fortified manor houses, 91
  as fortified residences, 15, 21, 23
  furnishings in, 26, 27–28, 32
  great halls in, 26–28, 30
  health care in, 29, 30, 70
  leisure activities in, 43–44, 48–50
  locations of, 24
  pets in, 52

  role of commoners in, 75–76
  self-sufficiency of, 24
  sewer systems in, 28–29
  sleeping arrangements in, 27, 71
  slighting of, 92
  structures within, 24–26, 30–31
  timekeeping in, 36
  towers in, 15–20, 85
  use of glass in, 27
  use of stone in, 18, 19, 20–21, 77
  use of water in, 18, 24, 28, 29–30, 38–39
  workers in, 22, 25–26, 36, 67–76
    benefits for, 71–72, 73, 75
    lower-class, 68, 70–71
    as unmarried men, 68
    upper-class, 67–70
    see also chatelaines; children; knights; nobles
catwalks, 84
Cesena Castle (Italy), 45
chain mail, 56, 60, 70
Château Gaillard (France), 87–88, 92
chatelaines, 45–48, 50
  appearance of, 46–47
  conflicting responsibilities of, 45, 46–47
  dowrys of, 45
  as health providers, 70
  as mothers, 50–51
chess, 44
Chester Castle (England), 25
children
  breastfeeding of, 50–51
  discipline of, 51, 53–54
  education of, 52–55
  as pages, 54–56

as servants, 70–71
church, 13, 38
    attendance at, 68
    on crossbows, 84–85
    on dancing, 48–49
    fast days and, 41
    on games of chance, 43–44
    on knighthood rituals, 58
    on marriage customs, 54
    mystery plays of, 49–50
    offerings to, 71
    schools of, 52
    on tournaments, 62
    on wet nurses, 50
    on women, 46
clergy, 13, 32–33, 34, 68
    clothing of, 36
clocks, 36
clothing, 35–36, 47, 59, 60
coat of arms, 64
colée, 58
Colmieu, Jean de, 15, 16, 23
common people, 11, 32–33
    clothing of, 36
    daily lives of, 35
    as knights, 58
    life expectancy of, 75
    revolts of, 69
    as servants, 68
    trials by ordeal and, 39
    as vagrants, 74
    during wartime, 75–76
concentric fortifications, 20, 77
Coulton, G. G., 39, 54, 83
crossbowmen, 84–85

Daily Life in the Middle Ages
    (Winston), 41
*Daily Living in the Twelfth
    Century* (Holmes), 21, 39,
    73
dancing, 48–49
Davis, William Stearns, 24, 30,
    70
Devizes Castle (England), 88
dice games, 43–44

Distant Mirror, A (Tuchman),
    33, 69
donjon (tower), 15, 17–18,
    19–20, 21, 26
drawbridges, 77, 78
dubbing, 57–58
Duby, Georges, 13, 65–66, 90
duels, 39

education, 52–55
Edward I (king of England), 87
England, 18–19, 20, 38, 65, 91
    barbarian tribes in, 10
    castles of, 18–19, 20, 24–25,
        75, 77, 88, 92
    feudal system in, 15
    kings of, 62, 77, 83, 85, 87,
        90–91, 92
    languages in, 48
    liquor consumption in, 39,
        72, 73
    money system in, 23
escalade, 77–79
Europe, 10, 15
Evans, Joan, 15, 34
*Everyday Life of Medieval
    Travelers* (Rowling), 22

farmers, 13, 34, 74, 75
feudalism, 11–14, 34, 89
    the church and, 13
    communication barriers and,
        48
    as economic system, 90
    family-like nature of, 13–14
    under William the Con-
        queror, 19
Feudal Society (Bloch), 48
First Crusade, 20
floggings, 38
flour mills, 69
food, 40–41, 69, 72
Fotheringhay Castle (En-
    gland), 24–25
France, 10, 20, 38, 65–66
    castles of, 86, 88–89, 91, 92
    dice games in, 44

feudal system in, 12–14, 15
    kings of, 90–91
    money system in, 21
    as wine producer, 39
Franks, 10, 12, 38
French combat, 61
Froissart, Jean, 63–64, 69, 86
Fry, Plantagenet Somerset, 21,
    23

games, 43–44, 48, 50, 51–52
gardens, 33, 70
garrisons (soldiers), 17, 18, 20
    during attacks, 84, 86
Gautier of Salins, 45
Gerald of Wales, 31–32
Germany, 11, 15
Gies, Frances, 60
girls, 47, 52, 54
gout, 29
grands seigneurs. See barons
Great Britain. *See* England
Greek fire, 80
Guesclin, Bertrand du, 75–76,
    78–79
Guibert (abbot), 53
gunpowder, 81

haircuts, 35
Hastings Castle (England),
    18–19
hauberks (armor), 59–60, 70
hawking, 43
health care practices, 29, 30,
    70
helmets, 60, 64
Henry II (king of England), 62
Henry III (king of England),
    92
heraldry, 64
Hohler, Christopher, 65
Holmes, Urban Tigner, Jr.
    on ale, 73
    on chess, 44
    on garderobes, 28–29
    on military training, 55
    on money, 21

on punishment of accused, 39

on vagrants, 74

homage rituals, 14

horses, 12, 25, 59

Hovedon, Roger de, 62

Hubert, Robert Fitz, 88

Hundred Years' War, 91

hunting, 41–43

illnesses, 29, 30, 70

Italy, 15, 45

Jacques of Vitry (monk), 33

James II (king of Scotland), 81–82

John of Toul (knight), 12

jury systems, 38

Kemp, Anthony, 18, 73, 78

knights, 14, 19, 64–66, 89

armor of, 59–60, 64, 84

as castle guards, 65–66

coat of arms for, 64

dubbing of, 57–58

duels and, 39

financial burdens of, 59–61, 65

as judges, 37

as landowners, 12, 13, 34

loyalty oaths of, 12

as prisoners, 30

shield money and, 65

tournaments for, 61–64, 83

training for, 55–57

wartime profits for, 60–61

knight's fee, 12

Krak des Chevaliers (Syria), 88, 92

Labarge, Margaret Wade, 24, 27, 29, 50, 60

ladies-in-waiting, 47–48

and *courtoisie,* 50

Lambert (priest), 16–17

lamps, 26

lances, 56

Lanercost Chronicle, 79, 84

languages, 47, 48, 52

legal systems, 38, 39

Legh, Bartholomew de, 60

Les quatre ages de l'homme (The Four Ages of Man), 34, 37, 46

Life in the Middle Ages (Coulton), 39, 54, 83

Life in the Middle Ages (Williams), 12

Limoges Castle (France), 86

lords, 12, 13–14

see also nobles

machicolations (stone galleries), 84

mail shirt (armor), 59–60

mangonel (stone thrower), 80, 84

manor houses, 17, 91

manorial system, 13

mantelet (movable shelter), 82

marriage customs, 54

Medieval Castle in England and Wales, The (Pounds), 92

melees, 62

Melun Castle, 78–79

mercenaries, 85, 89–90

Merlin Merlot (French tale), 75

Mertes, Kate, 37–38, 67, 68

mews (structure), 26

Middle Ages, The (Bishop), 29

military training, 55–57

miners, 82–83, 84

moats, 16, 24, 28, 77, 78, 84

money, 21, 65

monks. *See* clergy

mottes (fortified hill), 16–17, 19

murder holes, 84

musicians, 48

nobles, 11, 14, 32–44, 67

bloodletting of, 70

charity of, 37, 40, 41, 46, 68

clothing of, 35–36

income of, 20

as judges, 37–38, 90

leisure time of, 41–44

military training of, 55–57

personal habits of, 34–35

as vassals, 12, 34

view of peasants, 75

as warriors, 38, 90

Normans, 12, 15, 18–19, 38, 48

manor houses of, 17, 26

Nottingham Castle (England), 25

Ordelaffi, Marcia, 45

pages, 54–56

palisades, 15–16, 17, 19, 79–80

parapets, 85

parenting practices, 50–52

pavis (movable shelter), 82

Pax Romana, 10, 11

peasant class, 34, 73–76

see also common people

Perth Castle (Scotland), 88

pets, 52

Philip of Novara, 51

pillory, 38

Pisan, Christine de, 22

plays, 49–50

Pounds, N. J. G., 92

on castle warfare, 18, 77, 86, 87

on chapels, 30–31

Prestwich, Michael, 56, 59, 64, 85

prisoners, 30, 60, 63, 80

quintain (training device), 56

Regensburg, Berthold von, 47

Richard of Cornwell, 42

Richardson, H. G., 19

Richard I (king of England), 77, 85

Robert of Blois, 46

Roman Empire, 10–11

Rowling, Marjorie, 22
Roxburgh Castle (Scotland), 81–82
rushlight, 26

sallies, 85–86
sappers (miners), 82–83, 84
Saracen Castle (Spain), 20
Sayles, G. O., 19
seigneurial system, 13
serfs, 13, 34, 74, 75
sewer systems, 28–29
siege engines, 18, 80–81, 87
    names for, 80
soldiers. *See* garrisons; knights
spices, 70
squires, 56–58, 60
    dubbing of, 57–58
stewards, 38, 67–68
Stirling Castle (Scotland), 77, 80, 86–87, 92
stockings, 36, 59
stone throwers, 80, 81
storytellers, 48
sundials, 36
swords, 56–57

Thomas of Chantimpré, 42, 48
toilet paper, 29
tournaments, 61–64, 83
    financial rewards in, 63
Tower of London (England), 20, 92
towers, 15–20
    arrow slits in, 85
    height of, 16, 17
toys, 52
trebuchet (stone thrower), 80, 81, 84
trial by ordeal, 39
Tuchman, Barbara W., 33, 45
    on castles, 22
    on hawking, 43
    on medieval society, 11
    on peasant revolts, 69
    on the ranks of nobility, 34

undermining, 83–84

vagrants, 74
vassals, 12–14
    see also common people

Venette, Jean de, 75
Vikings, 10, 15
Vitalis, Ordericus, 18–19

warhorses, 12, 25, 59
Warwolf (siege engine), 80, 87
weapons, 25, 56–57
    crossbows, 81, 84–85
    lances, 56
    stone throwers, 80, 81
    swords, 56–57
wet nurses, 50–51
William of Malmesbury, 82
Williams, Jay, 12, 52, 57, 62, 89
William the Conqueror, 18–19
William the Marshal (knight), 63
wimples (head covering), 47
wine, 39
Winston, Clara and Richard, 11–12, 41
women, 39, 69, 84
    see also chatelaines

Ypres Castle (Belgium), 88

Picture Credits

Cover photo: Peter Newark's Historical Pictures
Corbis/Paul Almasy, 64
Corbis/Phil Schermeister, 32
National Library of Medicine, 29, 71

North Wind Picture Archives, 11, 19, 20, 21, 23, 25, 28, 31, 37, 49, 51, 59, 61, 74, 76, 79, 82, 87
Stock Montage, Inc., 13, 17, 27, 35, 40, 42, 43, 46, 47, 53, 57, 63, 67, 72, 85, 89, 91

About the Author

Gary L. Blackwood is a playwright, novelist, and nonfiction writer. He writes for adult and children's magazines on a wide range of subjects but specializes in history and biography. Many of his plays and novels are set in the past, from the twelfth century to the 1960s. His nonfiction books include a biography of Theodore Roosevelt, a book about life on the Oregon Trail, and a series that explores paranormal phenomena (ghosts, ESP, UFOs, reincarnation, etc.). He and his wife and two children live in the country near Carthage, Missouri.